3-D Butterfly Patterns in Peyote

Sheila Root, PhD
Master Jeweler

©2016 Sheila Root
rootsbeads@gmail.com

Text, designs, and photography ©2016 Sheila Root

All rights reserved. No portion of this work may be reproduced or used in any form or by any means -graphical, electronic, digital or mechanical including photocopying, photographing, recording, taping of information on storage and retrieval systems- without the written consent of the author.

The written instructions, photographs, designs and projects in this book are intended for the personal use of the reader, which would include making pieces to sell at local fairs or as gifts but not mass produced for sale through other venues such as internet sites or catalogs.

Sheila Root is a beading artist and was in the bead business for over twenty years before leaving to travel and write. She has taught hundreds of students in seed bead techniques and basic and advanced stringing techniques as well as wire techniques. A former university professor with degrees in design and a certificate in Master Jewelry, she has been designing and selling "wearable art" for many years. Sheila also has a background in textile arts and was a founding member of FiberRoots, participated in many gallery exhibitions both in group shows and as featured artist. She has written several other books including:

Graphics for Interior Space (out of print)
Beaded Ornament Covers: A Beginner's Guide
Beaded Ornament Covers Book Two
Beaded Ornament Covers Book Three
Handmade, not Homemade: A Bead Stringing Guide
Peyote Stitch for Beginner and Beyond
Spirit of the West: Amulet Bags in Peyote Stitch
A Butterfly Garden in Peyote Stitch.
Bird Patterns in Peyote Stitch
Wire Wrapping Stones and Beads (2nd Edition)

This book is one of a series of patterns for Peyote stitch. Watch for other titles coming soon.

Contents

Getting Started
Page....1

Red Admiral
Page... 13

Black Swallowtail
Page...17

Ruby Lacewing
Page...21

Janetta Forester
Page...25

Small Tortoiseshell
Page...29

Buckeye
Page...33

Purple Spotted Swallowtail
Page...37

Danube Clouded Yellow
Page...41

Corinna Daggertail
Page...45

Getting Started

The butterflies in this book are all designed to be three dimensional on the front but flat on the back. The flat back allows them to be used in a necklace, with a pin back to make a broach, added to a hairclip, framed, or any other application.

The butterfly shapes have freeform edges. Freeform shaped designs in peyote stitch involve using increases and decreases at the ends of rows to create a shape with no background. Most rows will also have an odd number of beads, requiring the use of odd count peyote stitch.

This book is not intended to teach you peyote stitch if you have never done it before. However the paragraphs below will give you a refresher on odd-count peyote stitch plus increases and decreases.

Odd Count Peyote

When working in odd count Peyote Stitch, there are two different ways of doing the odd-count ends of the rows. The edge will be nicer if you use Method 1 on the first odd-count row and then you can use Method 2 on the rest of the rows. If the edge starts getting a little out of line, do another row with Method 1.

Method 1: Start with stringing on the beads from row 1 and row 2 the same as in even count peyote stitch. The third row is worked the same as the third row in even count peyote stitch until you get to the last bead.

At the end of the third row it is necessary to take an extra stitch to anchor the last bead of row three and begin row four.

String on the next to last bead for row 3 (A) and run the needle back through the last bead from row 2 (B) and the end bead from row 1 (C) (right to left as shown).

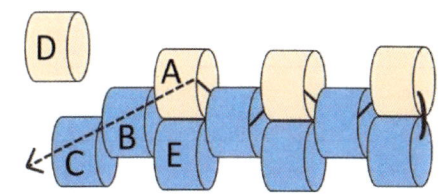

With the thread coming out of the end bead from row 1 (C), pick up the last bead for row 3 (D).

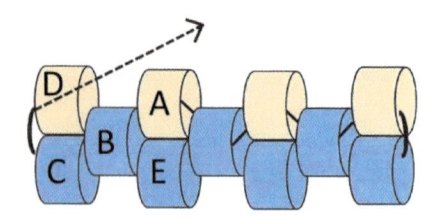

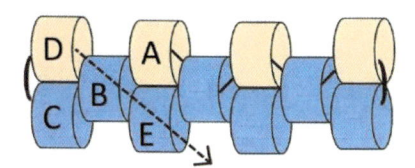

Run the needle down through the last bead of row 2 (B) and the second bead of row 1 (E).

With the thread coming out of E, run the needle right to left through A, B, and C.

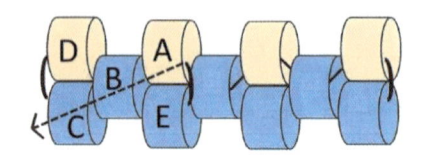

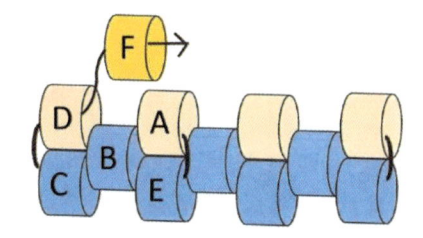

Run the needle left to right through D.

You are now ready to begin the 4th row (bead F).

If you put all the steps together in one diagram you can see that you are making a figure 8.

Remember that only one end of odd count peyote stich requires the extra stitch. The even numbered rows are started the same as in even count peyote. The odd numbered rows require the figure 8 stitch or Method 2, shown below.

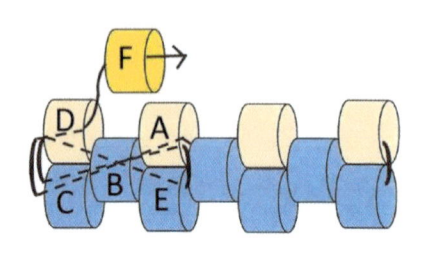

Continue adding rows. The extra figure 8 stitch has anchored the end bead.

Method 2: When working a rectangular piece of odd count peyote stitch, using a figure eight pattern at the end of all the rows gives a nicer edge to the work. However, in freeform designs the odd count sections are usually quite short between increases and decreases. It is easier to use this simpler method of adding the end bead on odd count rows after you have anchored the first one with the figure 8 from Method 1.

1. After adding bead A, exit through the last two beads (B & C) of the two previous rows (shown right to left)
2. Add the last bead (D) of the current row (shown in peach)
3. Loop back through the last bead (C) from the row below the D bead (shown right to left)
4. Run the needle through the new bead (D) again (shown left to right)
5. You are now ready to start the next row (E).

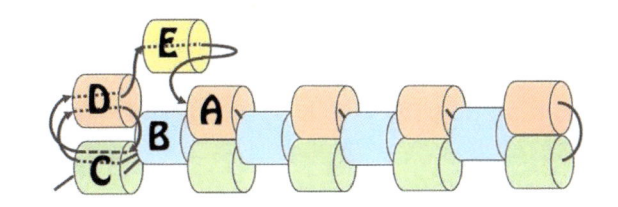

Increases and Decreases

Because there are so many increases and decreases, we want to keep them as simple as possible. Most increases and decreases will be only one column (one bead width) at a time. The location of increases are marked on the diagrams by < or >.

To increase by one column on an even count row:

1. At the end of the even count row where you need to increase, exit from the last bead of the previous row (B)
2. String on the two new beads (C & D). If the beads are different colors, check your diagram to make sure you have them in the correct order before step 5 and 6.
3. Run the needle back through bead B.
4. Exit from bead B on the left.
5. Run the needle through bead E and C (left to right as shown).
6. Run the needle back through bead D (right to left as shown).
7. Exit from bead D. You are now ready to begin the next row.

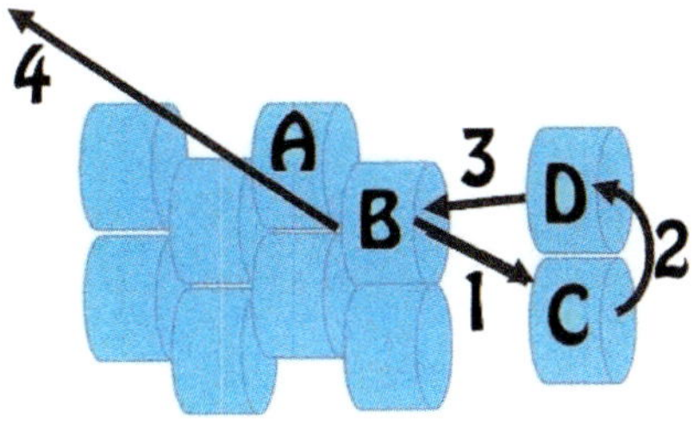

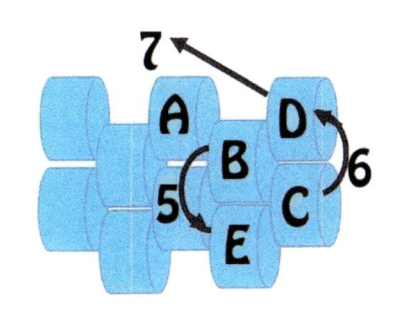

To increase by one column on an odd count row:

To increase on the end of an odd count row, it is easier to make the increase at the end of the odd count row above the row where you need the increase. To increase at the end of the row ending in bead C as shown here, first work the row beginning with B (left to right) and the row ending with A (right to left).

1. When you add the next to last bead of the top row (A), run the needle down through both B and C.
2. String on bead D. (thread not shown)
3. Run the needle right to left through bead C.
4. String on bead E and bead F.
5. Run the needle through bead C (left to right as shown).
6. Run the needle through bead D and F (right to left as shown).
7. You are now ready to add bead G to begin the next row.

This sounds much more complicated than it really is. After a couple of odd count increases you will get the hang of it! Note that the new row now begins like an even count row. As you work increases and decreases the piece will frequently change back and forth between odd count and even count ends.

To decrease by one column on an even count row: This method reduces the number of thread passes through beads.

1. Exit the even count row through the last bead of the previous row, bead B as you would normally.
2. Run the needle <u>under</u> the loop of thread between beads B and C.
3. Run the needle up through beads B and A (right to left).

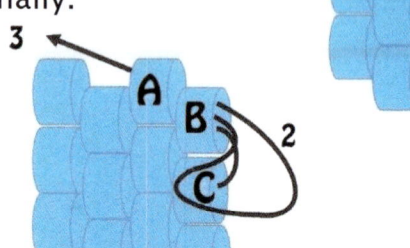

When you pull the thread up tight, if bead A falls off you will know that you didn't go <u>under</u> the loop! Put bead A back on and try again.

To decrease by one column on an odd count row:

This is the simplest method to decrease on an odd count row. Leave off the bead that would normally be added to fit above bead C.

Run the needle <u>under</u> the thread between beads B and C (arrow)

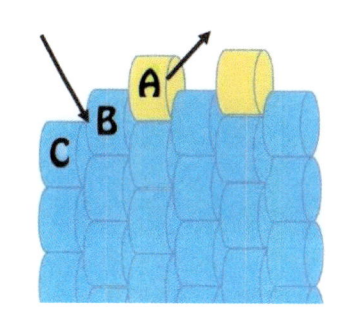

Run the needle back up through beads B and A. You are now ready to begin the next row.

Freeform shaped designs are constantly changing shape as you work, and because butterflies are symmetrical creatures, there will be an odd count finish, an increase or a decrease on most of the rows. As a result, odd count finishes will not necessarily all be on the same side of the design.

On some rows, if you were working the row from left to right, it would be a simple even count to finish the row and begin the next row above. However, if you need to work this row from right to left then you would have to treat it as a decrease and then the next row above would be an even count when worked back left to right.

Following Diagrams

If you are making a rectangular piece in peyote stitch you can simply start at one end and work to the other end. With freeform shaped designs in peyote stitch it is easier to start in the middle and work one direction, then go back and work the other direction. Most people find decreases easier to do than increases. Decreases are also a little easier to follow in a diagram for proper location.

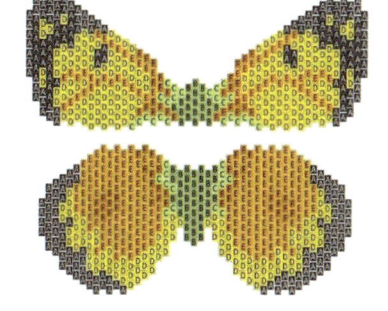

The patterns in this book are shown in two forms, a complete diagram and a divided chart that takes you through the design in sections and assembles the sections. Use the complete diagram if you wish to work in **Brick Stitch** rather than peyote stitch. You will still need to connect the two halves of the body when you have finished the beadwork on the wings.

Be sure to lay your ruler across the chart to make sure you stay on the same row, and check off each row as you progress so you don't accidentally miss a row or get an extra one.

Section Diagrams: If you are relatively new to increases, decreases, and freeform shapes in peyote stitch it will be easier for you to follow the divided chart instructions.

Each pattern is divided into sections to make it easier to follow the irregular shape. The sections are designed to reduce the number of increases. Each section is shown oriented in the direction of work from the bottom up.

For example, the butterfly shown in the complete pattern example on page 5 would be worked in four sections:

Section 1 is worked right side up, starting in the middle of a wide part of the butterfly.

Section 1 is then turned up side down so that Section 2 can be worked right side up. The thread is attached to Section 1 and the first row of Section 2 is worked into the first row of Section 1 so it becomes one piece.

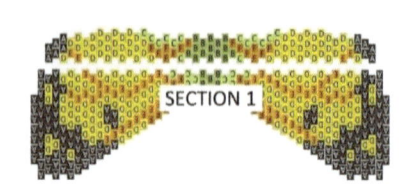

Section 3 is stated as a new piece, working bottom to top.

Section 3 is then turned over and the first row of Section 4 is worked into the first row of Section 3 creating one piece.

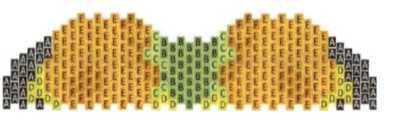

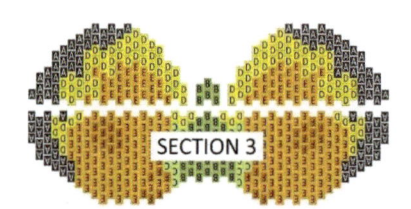

When the two halves are completed they are sewn together in the middle.

All the butterflies are symetrical and reversible so you don't have to worry about whether you are looking at the front or the back of each half.

Only connect the three "body" beads in the center of each half. Sew the two sections together: Run your thread back and forth from one side to the other, "zipping" up the seam. As you pull the thread snug the seam will disappear. Go back through the beads in both directions to secure the seam.

When the body is sewn together, the wings will overlap. The joint will seem a bit floppy, but it will be reinforced when you add the 3-D body to the front.

Adding the 3-D Body

The diagrams used to illustrate the body are shown with the cylinder beads in yellow. The blue cylinder beads represent the beads in the wings on either side of the body. If the wing beads get in the way of running the needle through a body bead, bend the wings back gently to expose the body bead a little more.

The small oval beads shown in tan are the 15/0 rocaille (round) beads that form the front of the body. Not everyone likes to work with the small 15/0 rocailles, but they are the best choice for the body. Cylinder beads with their flat ends don't curve nicely and larger rocailles are just too big and out of proportion with the rest of the butterfly.

The body is worked in peyote stitch with all rows running from left to right.

Row 1: The thread should be exiting the center cylinder bead in the body (B) from the left side.

Add one 15/0 (1) and run the needle back right to left through the same cylinder bead (B).

Row 2: String on one 15/0 (2), run through bead (1) and string on bead (3).

Run the thread right to left through bead B and bead A.

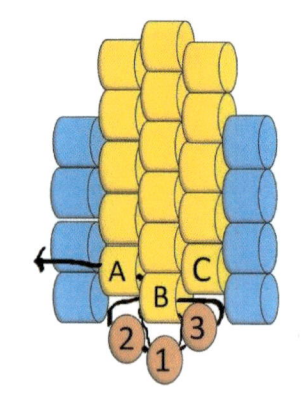

Row 3: String on bead 4, run through bead 2.

String on bead 5, run through bead 3.

String on bead 6. Run thread right to left through bead C, skip over bead B, and exit right to left through Bead A. (The thread going over bead B will never be seen and this is easier than going through it.)

Row 4: Run the thread up through Bead 4 from Row 3.

String on Bead 7, run through Bead 5.

String on Bead 8, run through Bead 6.

Run the thread right to left through the same Bead C as the previous row. Skip over Bead B, exit through the next Bead A above the one used in the previous row.

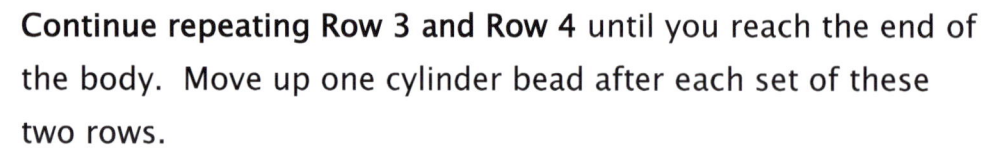

Continue repeating Row 3 and Row 4 until you reach the end of the body. Move up one cylinder bead after each set of these two rows.

When you reach the head area you can make eyes by replacing the beads in the 7 and 8 position with an 11/0 rocaille.

Make one last row with 15/0 rocailles after the eyes, exiting through the B Bead at the point of the head.

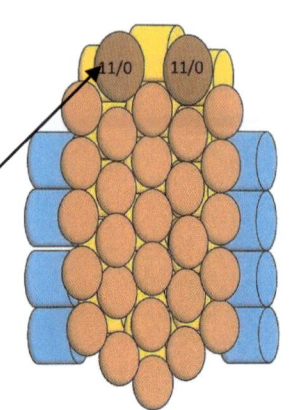

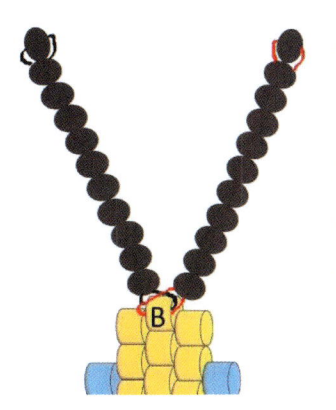

Antennae: String on about 12 15/0 rocailles (diagram shows 10).

String on one more 15/0 and run the needle back down through the 12 beads and into the opposite side of the B Bead. Repeat for the second one.

Press the completed body a little from each side to fatten him up. The finished body will have a kind of honeycomb effect.

Needles and Thread

Peyote stitch in general can be pretty hard on the thread, but working all the decreases, increases, and odd count ends is even tougher on your thread. Choose a high quality beading thread in a relatively fine weight. For a normal piece of rectangular even count peyote stitch a size D or 8 lb. thread and a size 10 needle work fine, but they are too thick for this kind of work.

Choose about a **4 lb. weight in a braided thread or a size AA in a flat beading thread**. The flat beading threads come in beautiful colors to compliment your beads, however, they are more delicate than braided thread. If the thread starts to fray too much, end it and start a new piece. Thread conditioner may help keep your thread from fraying as much.

Also choose a smaller size needle, no larger than a **size 11 or 12**, especially for the 3-D body. Either beading needles or sharps work well. The sharps bend less. Working increases and decreases requires extra passes of the needle through many end beads and if your needle is too thick it can get stuck in a bead. If the needle won't go through a bead, pull it off and use a smaller size needle. Don't force the needle through since this can break the bead, especially if it is a matt finish bead. The matt finish beads seem to break easier than the shiny ones.

Make sure you are using a needle no larger than size 12 for the body. The cylinder beads along the edges of the body will have several passes of thread.

Beads

All the patterns in the book are sized for 11/0 Japanese cylinder beads. The color numbers given are for Miyuki Delica beads. The patterns can also be worked in other brands of Japanese cylinder beads but their numbers will be different.

The patterns could be worked in 15/0 cylinder beads for a more delicate version or in 10/0 cylinder beads for a larger version. Using 11/0 rocailles (round seed beads) instead of cylinder beads would distort the shape of the finished piece since the length to width ratio is not the same as it is for the cylinder beads.

Tip: Before you begin beading, **get organized**. It is much easier to keep track of your bead colors if you use a beading tray and label the bins A, B, C, etc. to match the color numbers on the charts.

Lay your ruler across the row you are working on in the diagram. Pick the colors from the beading dish and lay them out in order on your bead mat. Check off the row on the chart. Work the row from the line of beads on the mat. Repeat for the next row.

Substituting Colors

If you are unable to find the colors used in the patterns it may sometimes be necessary to substitute colors. A lot of trial and error has gone into selecting colors for the patterns because some colors or finishes just don't work well in this type of use.

Keep in mind that many colors and/or finishes look very different worked up than they do in the tube. Transparent colors, especially the lighter ones, may look like the right color in the tube but when they are worked into a pattern they look much lighter and often washed out. Some color numbers may look like two totally different shades in the tubes but when they are worked side by side the difference is so subtle that they look the same. Subtle color changes add realism as long as you can see them.

Also maintain a balance of shiny and matte colors. Some designs can look a little flat if the whole thing is worked in matte finishes, but with all shiny beads the pattern can just get lost in the shine. Duracoat colors work well. They have a subtle sheen to them that shows off the pattern without looking dull.

Test your substitute colors before working up the whole design. String about two beads of each color onto a needle in the order they will be in the pattern. If they don't look good on the needle they will definitely not look good in the pattern. If they look good on the needle, try working a tiny swatch of the colors together. If they still look good, go for it.

Changing Colors

Sometimes you may want to change the entire color of a butterfly to match a particular color scheme. Select the new colors in the same value range as the suggested colors: i.e. replace lightest color with the lightest shade in the new color and the darkest color with the darkest shade in the new color.

Body Colors

Suggested body colors are given in the material list, however they are not listed by color numbers. There are several manufacturers who make 15/0 rocailles and any of them will work even though they have some slight size variation.

If possible, work the wing sections first and then see which of your 15/0 colors look best with it. Matte AB colors work well for bodies because most butterfly bodies are rather fuzzy.

Choose an 11/0 for the eyes if desired. Shiny dark colors work best here. Most of the samples use either black, dark blue metallic AB, or brown metallic AB.

Abbreviations Used in Color Names

AB= aurora borealis   OP=Opaque   MAT=matte   TR=transparent
IRIS=rainbow finish   MET=metallic   DURA=duracoat   WID=white inside lined
S/L=silver lined

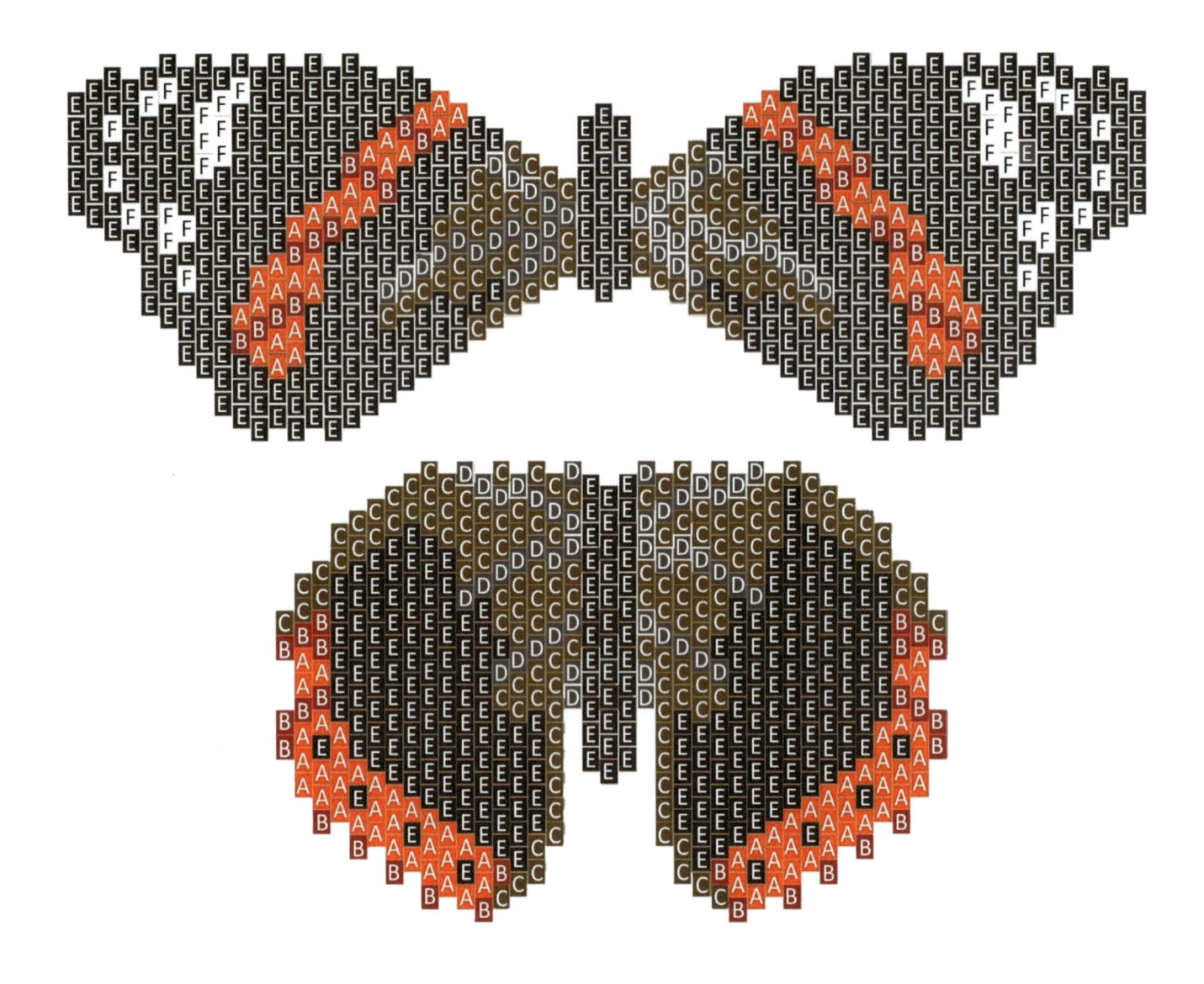

The Red Admiral is native to Europe and North America.

Red Admiral
(Vanessa Atalanta)

Materials:

Japanese Cylinder Beads

	Color #	Color Name	# of Beads
A	DB0722	Persimmon: OP MAT	120
B	DB0727	Siam Lt: OP	52
C	DB0735	Milk Chocolate Dk: OP	192
D	DB0306	Slate: MET MAT	78
E	DB0200	Black: OP	667
F	DB0010	White: OP	32

BODY: shown in 15/0 IRIS GRAY MATTE (TOHO brand)
ANTENNAE: 15/0 BLACK OP

Approximate Finished Size: 3" x 1 7/8" (76mm x 48mm)

Section 1:

Work from the bottom up following the diagram below.
Complete rows 1-3 and then work each wing and the body separately.

Row 1

Section 2:

Turn Section 1 over and work Section 2 into the first row of Section 1 following the diagram shown next.

13

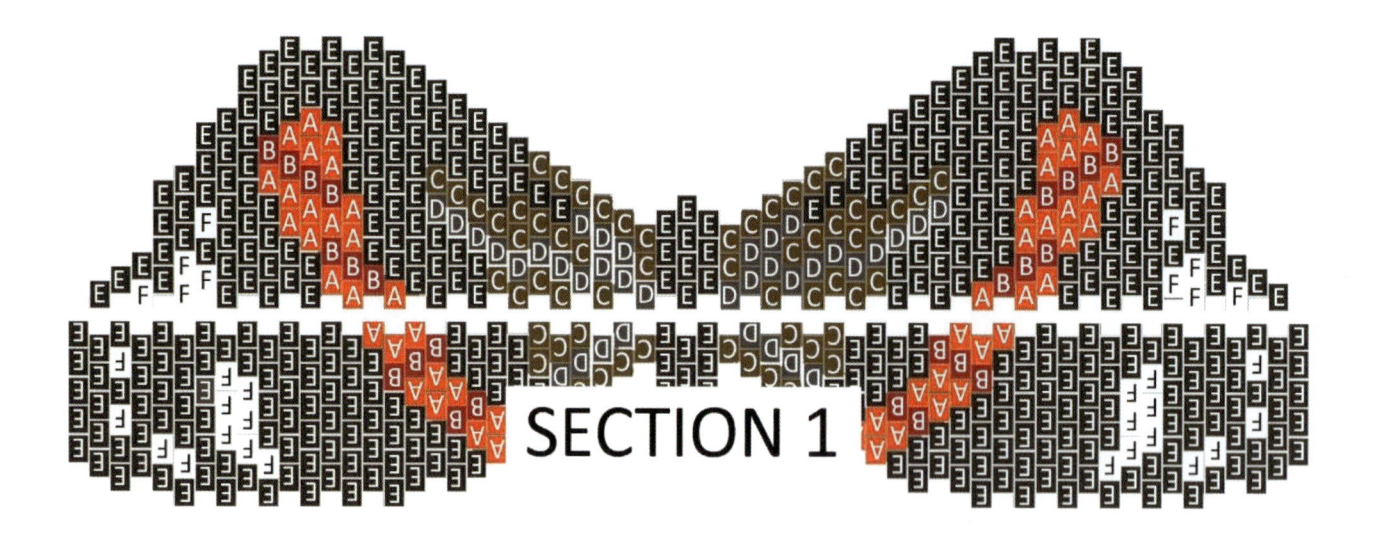

Section 3:

Work Section 3 from the bottom up following the diagram below. Match the decreases to the diagram and the increases to the < and > symbols.

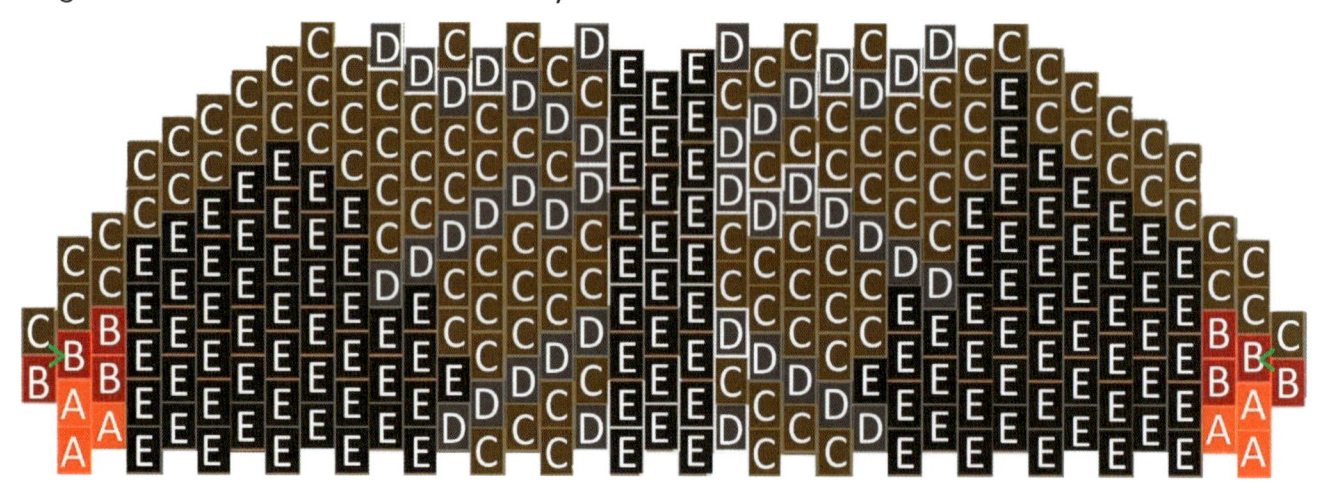

Section 4:

Turn Section 3 over and work Section 4 into the first row of Section 3 following the diagram shown next.

Work both wing tips. Do NOT work the body area of Section 4 just yet.

Wait on body

SECTION 3

Finish (refer back to Chapter 1, if needed):

When both halves are finished except for the tail end of the body, line up the two halves and sew them together at the body. Be careful to only sew the center three beads from each half.

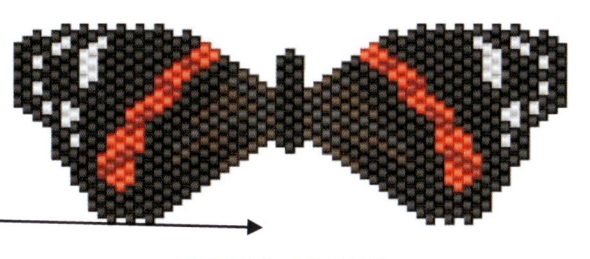

Add a new thread:

1. work the end of the base layer of the body from the wings down to the tail end
2. work the 3-D body from the tail end to the head end.
3. finish with the antennae.

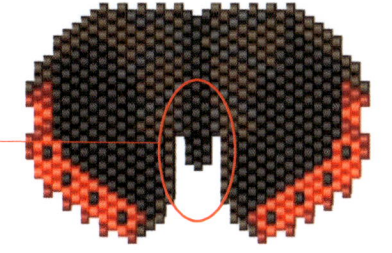

15

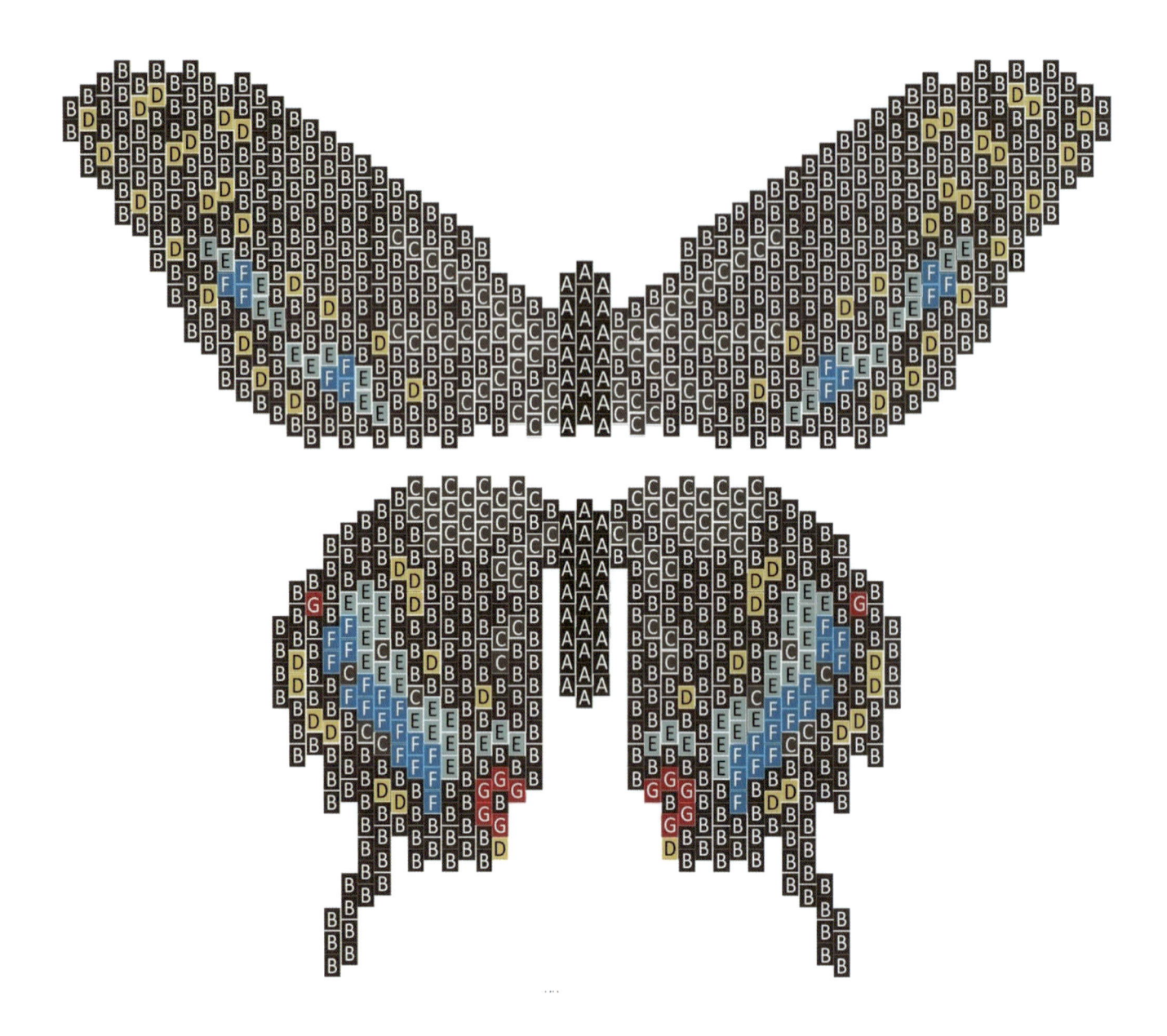

The Black Swallowtail lives from southern Canada to South America.

Black Swallowtail
(Papilio Polyxenes)

Materials:

Japanese Cylinder Beads

	Color #	Color Name	# of Beads
A	DB0010	Black: OP	44
B	DB0310	Black: OP MAT	724
C	DB0306	Slate: MET MAT	120
D	DB2101	Pale Yellow: OP DURA	58
E	DB1784	Baby Blue: WID	60
F	DB2135	Imperial Bl Dk: OP DURA	46
G	DB0722	Persimmon: OP	12

BODY: 15/0 BLACK OP
　　　 15/0 WHITE OP
ANTENNAE: 15/0 BLACK OP

Approximate Finished Size: 3" x 2 3/8" (76mm x 60mm)

Section 1:

Work Section 1 from the bottom up following the diagram below. Match decreases to the diagram and increases to the < and > marks. Complete the first three rows all the way across and then work each part separately.

Section 2:

Turn Section 1 over and work Section 2 into the first row of Section 1 following the diagram below.

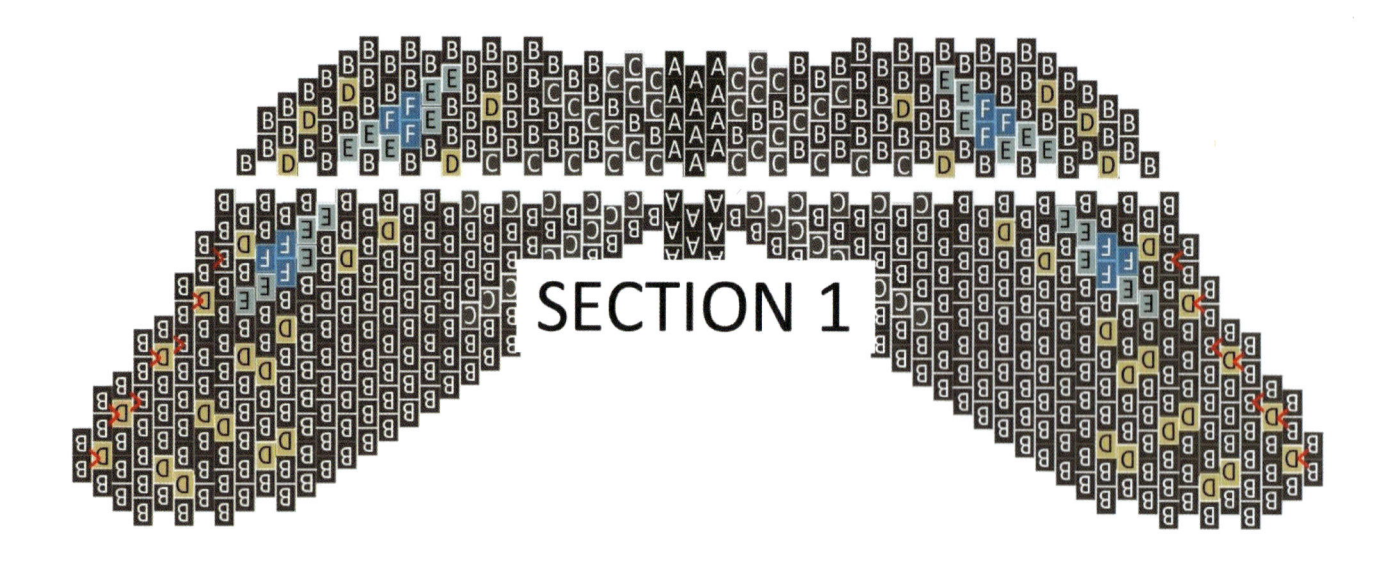

Section 3:

Work Section 3 from the bottom up following the diagram below.

Section 4:

Turn Section 3 over and work Section 4 into the first row of Section 3 following the diagram shown next. Work the two wing tips first and leave off the center section of the body for now. Match the increases and decreases to the diagram.

Note that the first row of each wing is worked straight up from Section 3 and then there are increases on rows 2, 3 and 6.

SECTION 3

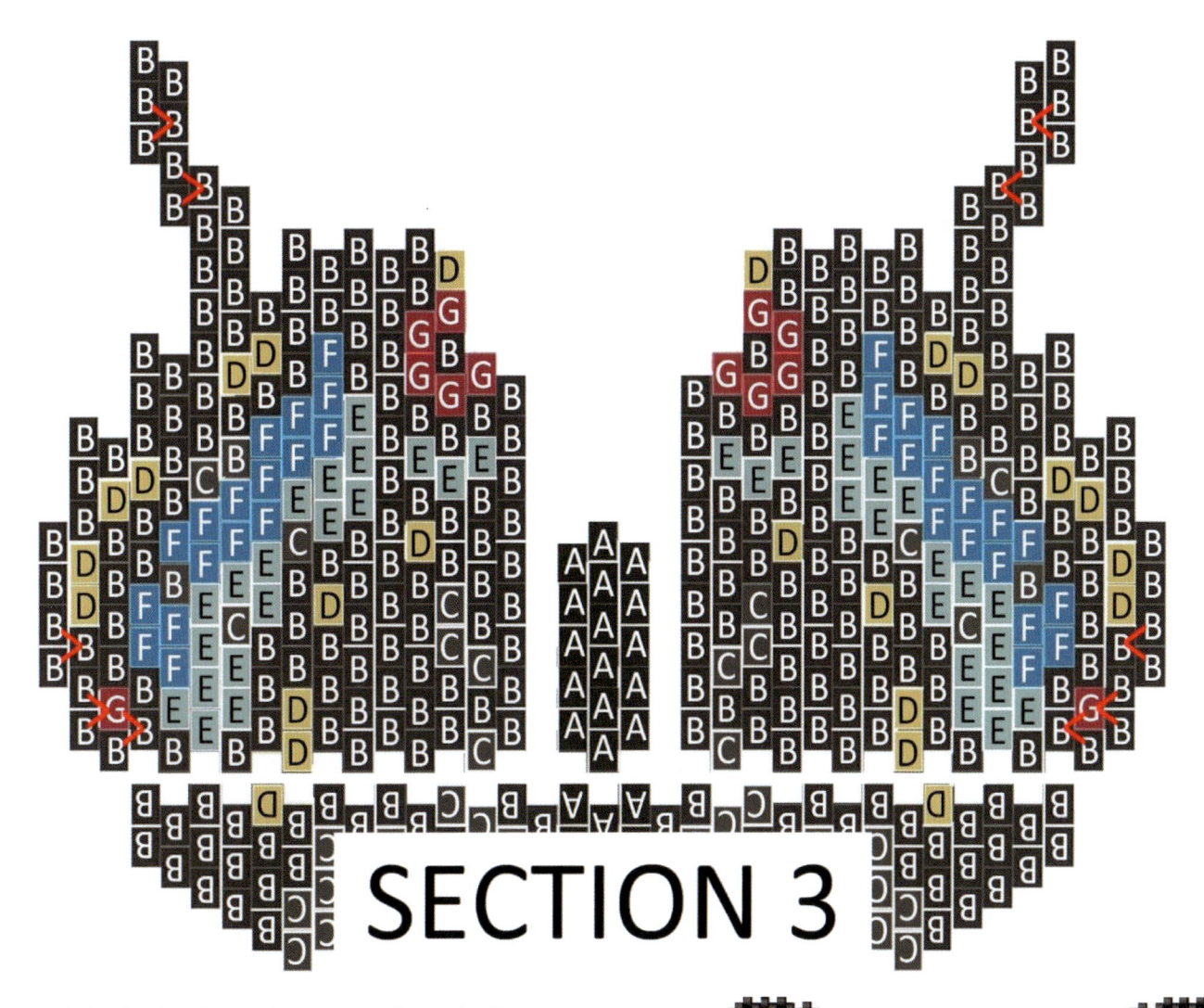

Finish (refer back to Chapter 1, if needed):

When both halves are finished except for the tail end of the body, line up the two halves and sew them together at the body. Be careful to only sew the center three beads from each half.

Add a new thread:

1. work the end of the base layer of the body from the wings down to the tail end
2. work the 3-D body from the tail end to the head end *
3. finish with the antennae.

*Add white spots to the back in the second and fourth bead position on every fourth peyote row in the tail end of the body and the back of the head.

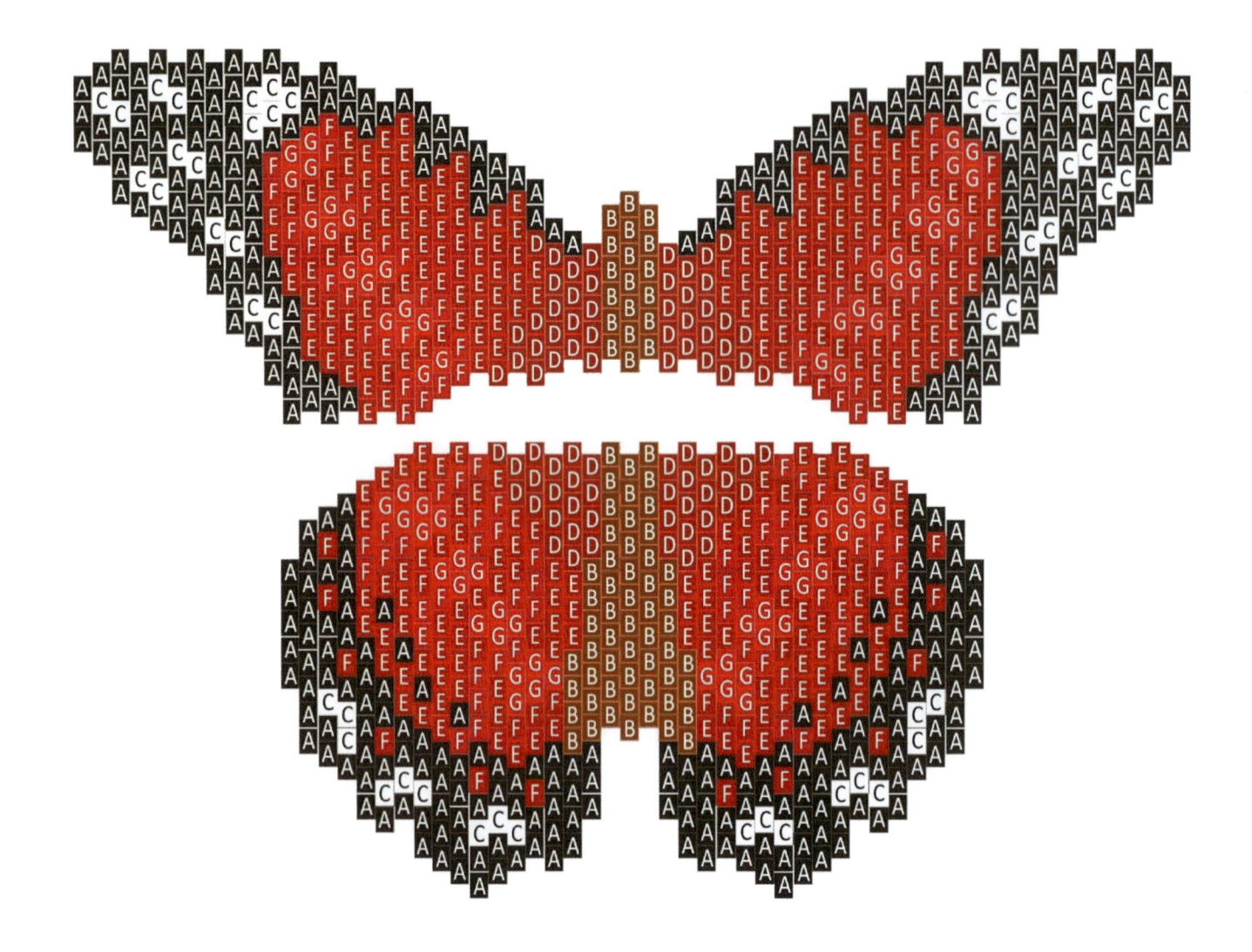

The Ruby Lacewing can be found in Indonesia, southeast Asia, and the Philippines.

Ruby Lacewing
(Cethosia Biblis)

Materials

Japanese Cylinder Beads

	Color #	Color Name	# of Beads
A	DB0310	Black: OP MAT	380
B	DB2108	Copper: OP DURA	74
C	DB200	White: OP	52
D	DB378	Mexican Red: OP MAT	78
E	DB0602	Ruby Red: S/L	283
F	DB0723	Red: OP	106
G	DB0159	Red Lt: OP AB	73

BODY: 15/0 BROWN MATTE
ANTENNAE: 15/0 BLACK OP

Approximate Finished Size: 3" x 2" (76mm x 50mm)

Section 1:

Work Section 1 from the bottom up following the diagram below, matching up the decreases and increases (marked by < and >). The first four rows are worked all the way across and then each wing and the center body piece are worked separately.

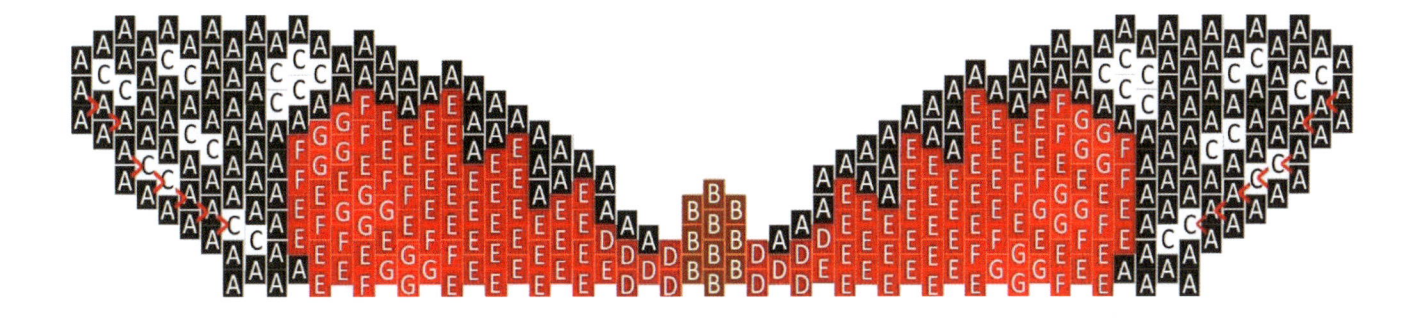

Section 2:

Turn Section 1 over and work Section 2 into the first row of Section 1 following the diagram below. Match location and decreases to the diagram.

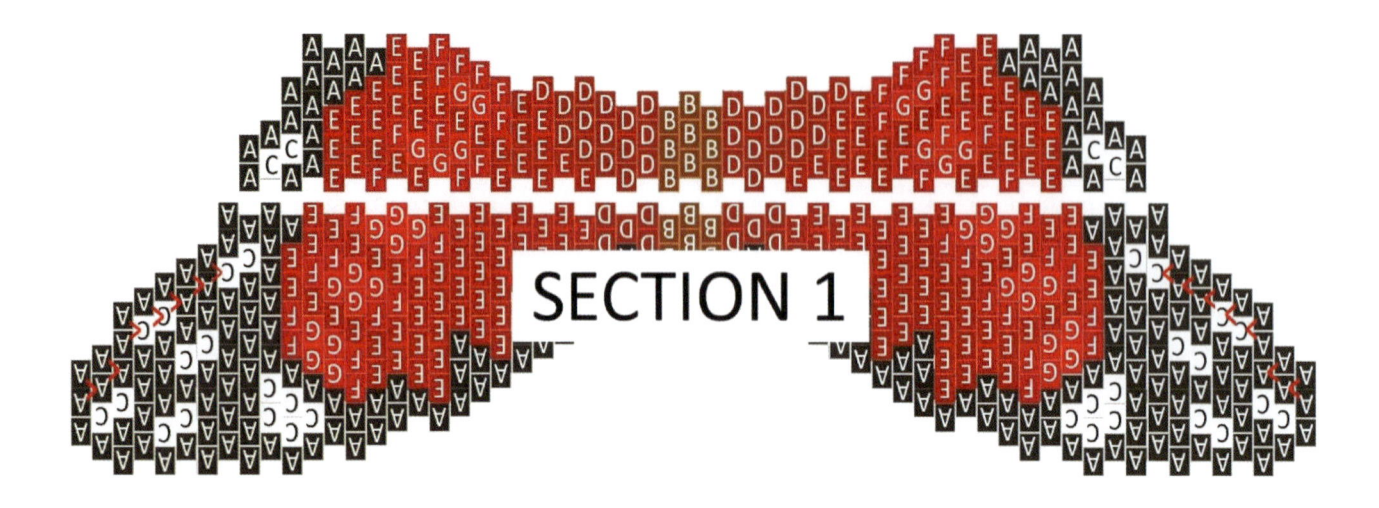

Section 3:

Work Section 3 from the bottom up following the diagram below.

Section 4:

Turn Section 3 over and work Section 4 into the first row of Section 3 following the diagram on the opposite page. After the first four rows, work the wing tips separately.

SECTION 3

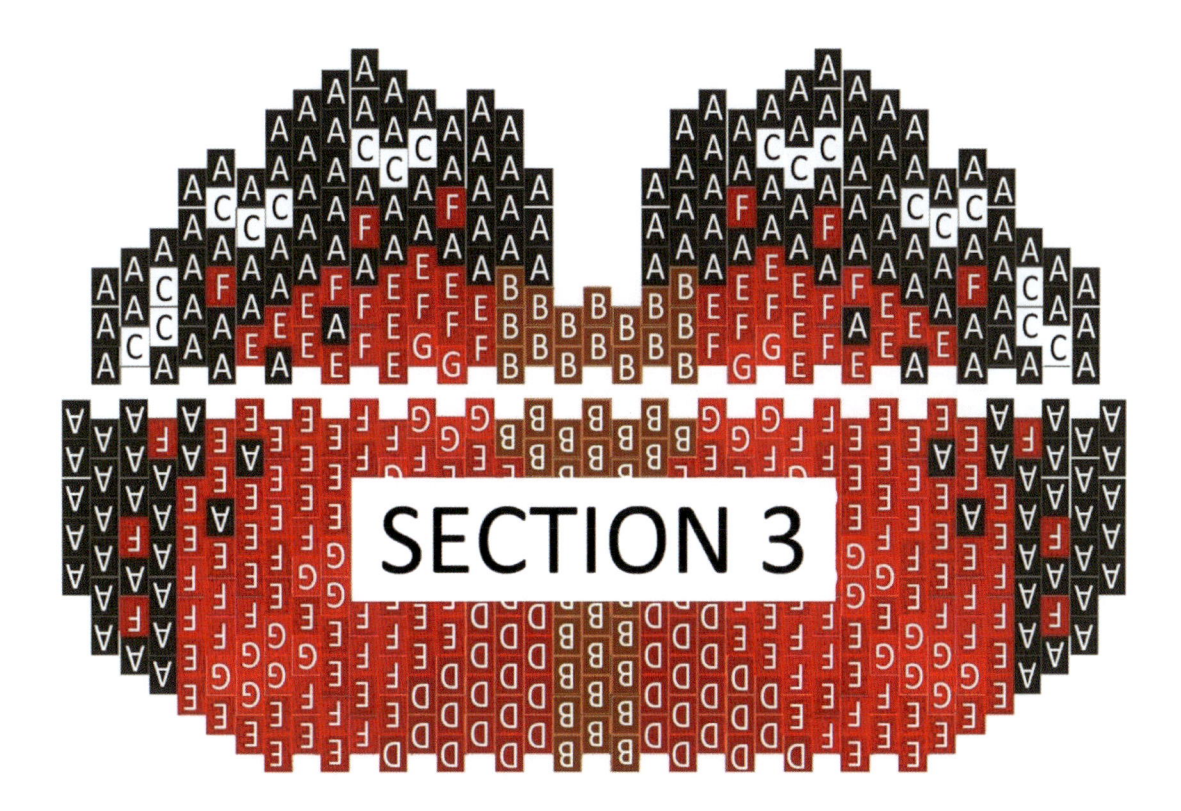

Finish (refer to Chapter 1, if needed):

When both halves are finished, line up the two halves and sew them together at the body. Be careful to only sew the center three beads from each half.

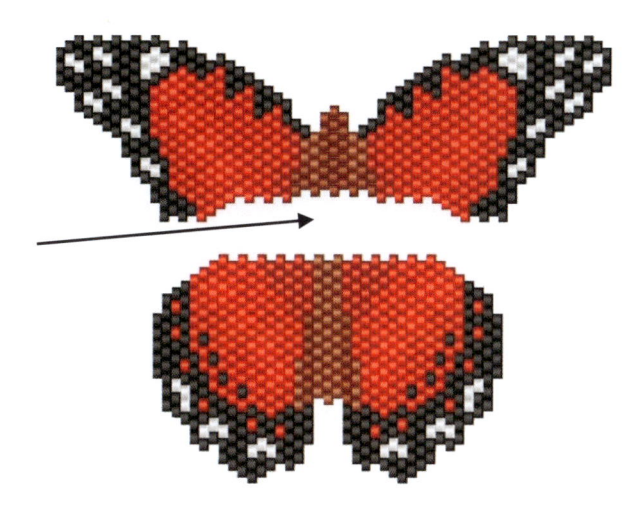

Add a new thread and work the 3-D body from the tail up and finish with the antennae.

23

The Janetta Forester butterfly lives in the forested areas of Africa.

Janetta Forester
(Euphaedra Janetta)

Materials:

Japanese Cylinder Beads

	Color #	Color Name	# of Beads
A	DB0002	Blue Black: MET IRIS	585
B	DB2135	Imperial Blue Dk: OP DURA	396
C	DB2132	Cadet Blue Dk: OP DURA	216
D	DB2129	Cadet Blue Lt: OP DURA	106
E	DB2102	Gold Lt: OP DURACOAT	70
F	DB1572	Lemon: OP AB	38
G	DB2120	Maroon Dk: OP DURACOAT	8

BODY: 15/0 DK BLUE IRIS MATTE
      WITH BLACK MATTE STRIPES (optional)
ANTENNAE: 15/0 BLACK MATTE

Approximate Finished Size: 3" x 2.25" (76mm x 57mm)

Section 1:

Work Section 1 from the bottom up following the diagram below. Match the decreases and increases (marked with < or >) to the diagram.

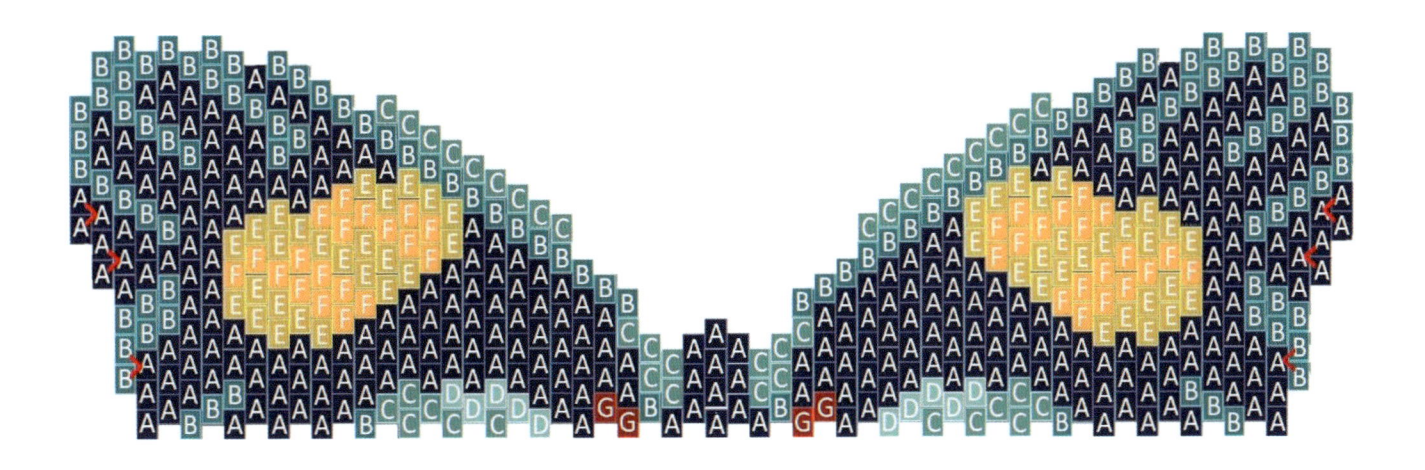

Section 2:

Turn Section 1 over and work Section 2 into the first row of Section 1 following the diagram below. Match the location and decreases to the diagram.

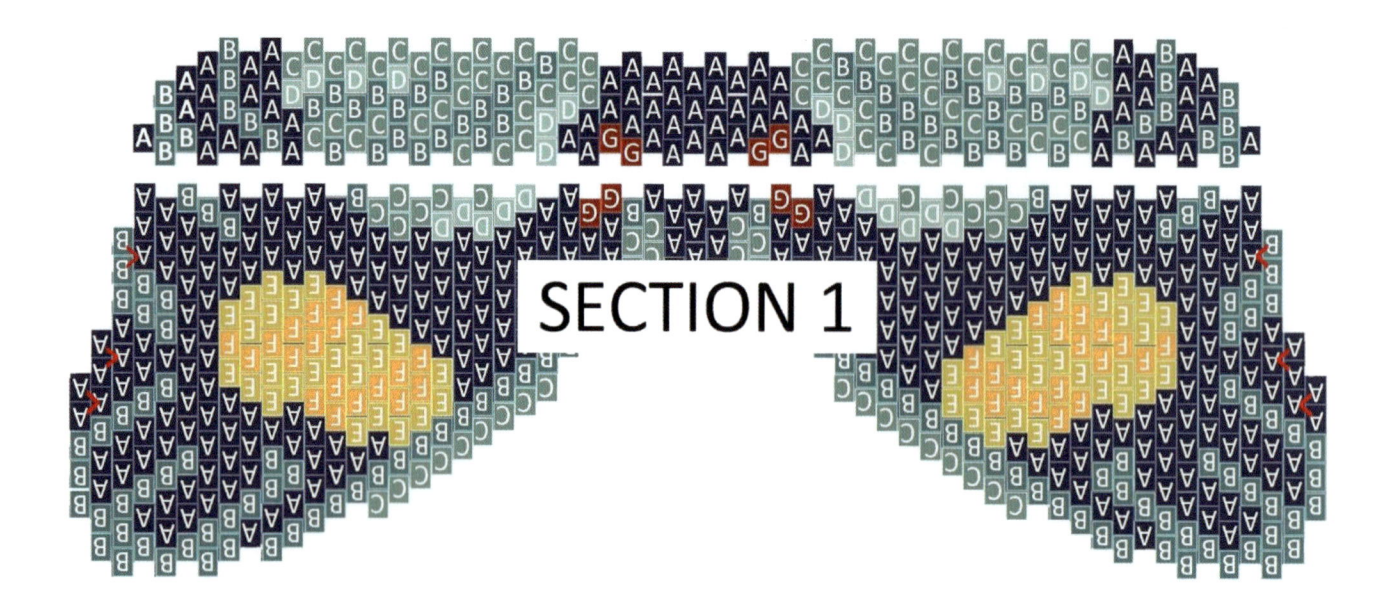

Section 3:

Work Section 3 from the bottom up following the diagram below. Match the decreases to the diagram. Work one wing tip then the other. Leave the end of the body section off until you are ready to work the top 3-D layer of the body.

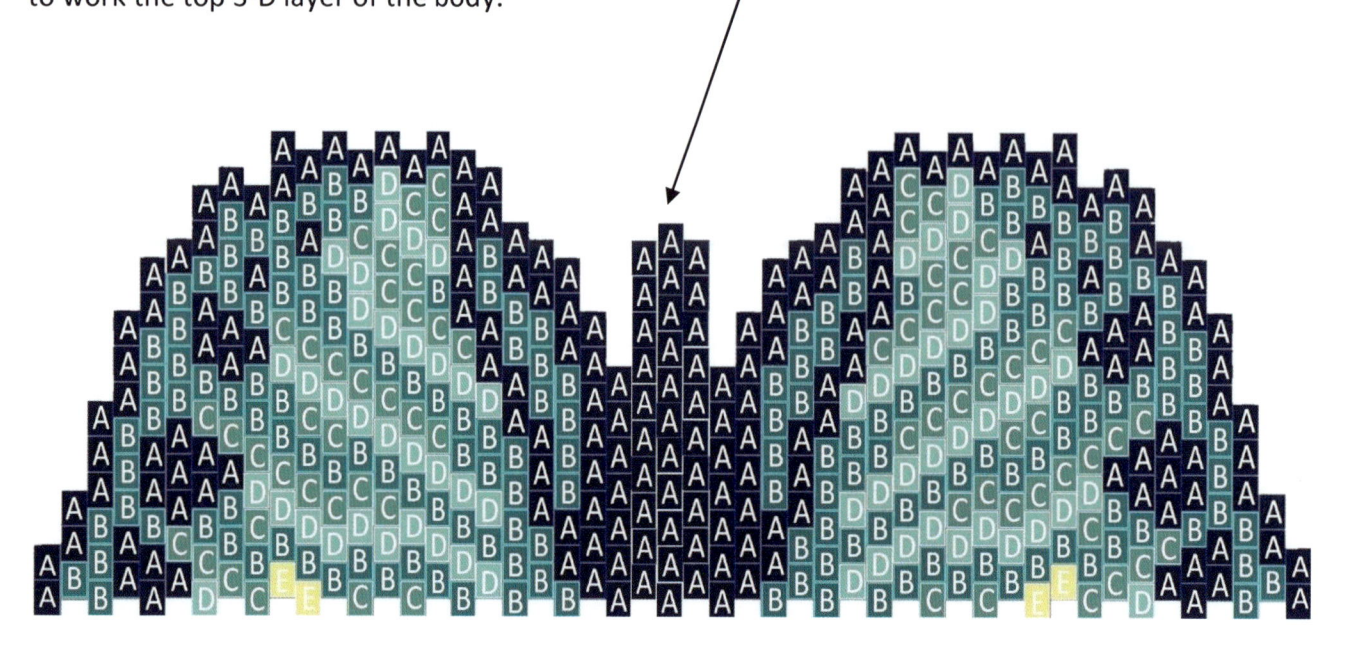

Section 4:

Turn Section 3 over and work Section 4 into the first row of Section 1 following the diagram below.

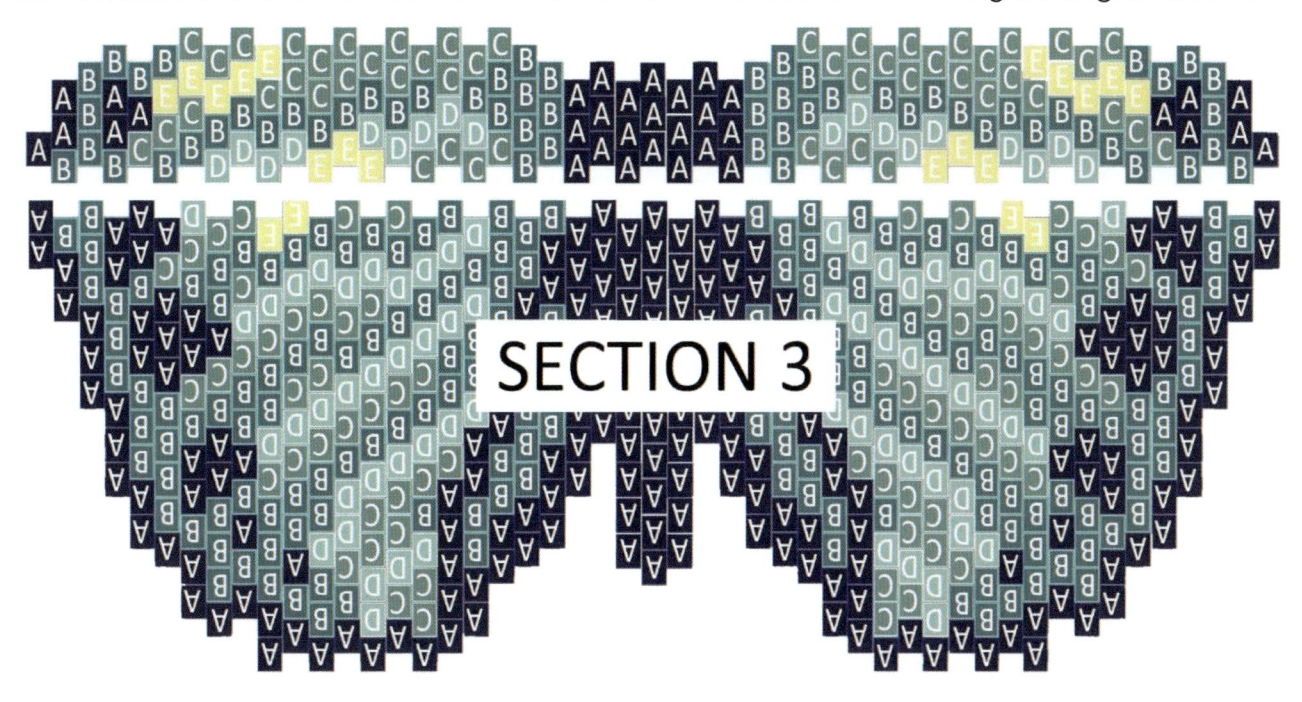

Finish (refer to Chapter 1, if needed):

When both halves are finished except for the tail end of the body, line up the two halves and sew them together at the body. Be careful to only sew the center three beads from each half.

Add a new thread:

1. work the end of the base layer of the body from the wings down to the tail end
2. work the 3-D body from the tail end to the head end.
3. finish with the antennae.

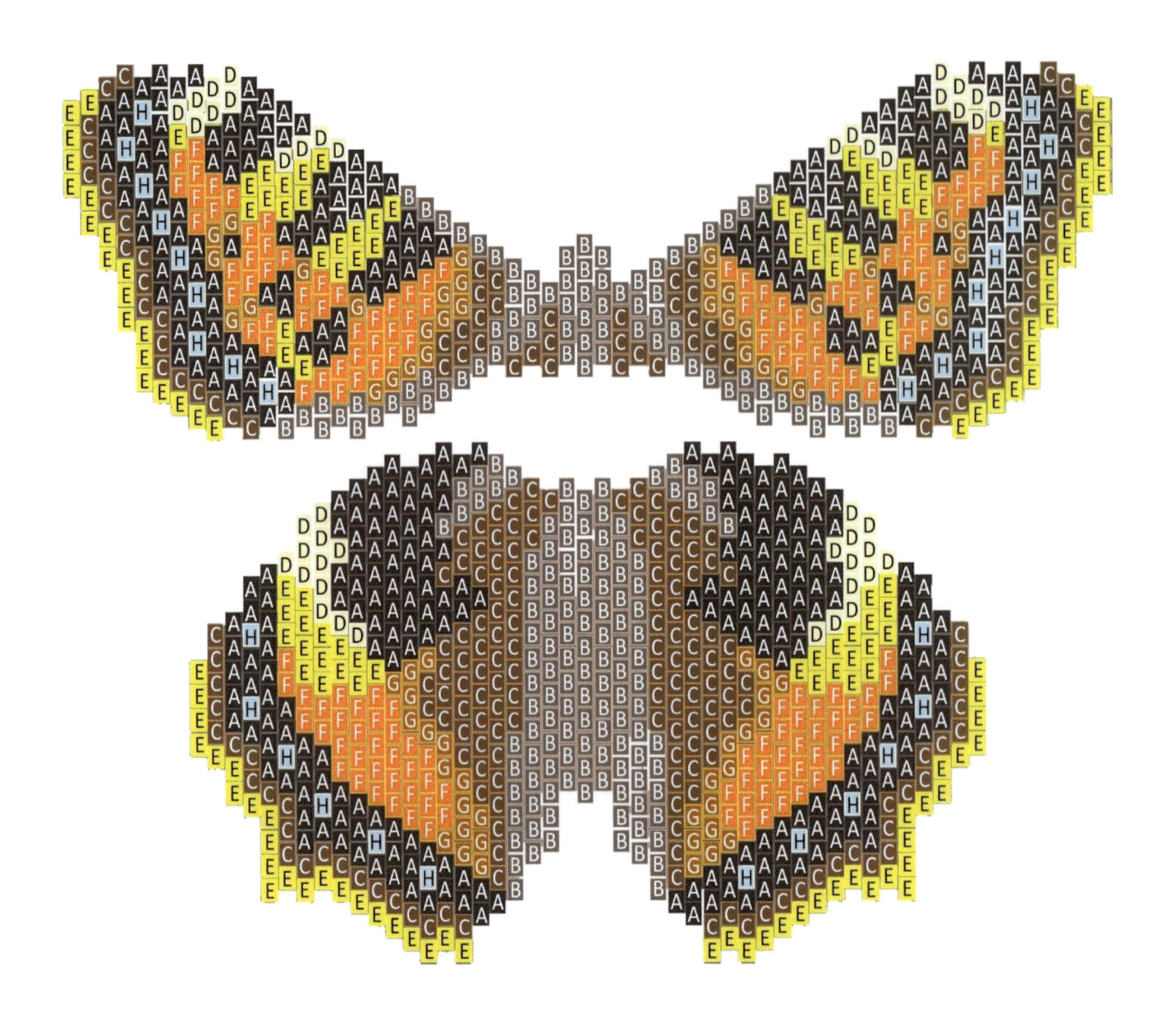

The Small Tortoiseshell butterfly lives in the temperate areas of Europe and Asia but is in rapid decline.

Small Tortoiseshell
(Aglais Urticae)

Materials:

Japanese Cylinder Beads

	Color #	Color Name	# of Beads
A	DB0310	Black: OP MAT	411
B	DB0735	Milk Chocolate Dk: OP	203
C	DB0865	Forest Brown: TR MAT AB	225
D	DB2101	Pale Yellow: OP DURA	46
E	DB1572	Lemon: OP AB	157
F	DB0722	Persimmon: OP	157
G	DB2108	Copper: OP DURACOAT	66
H	DB1784	Baby Blue: WID	30

BODY: 15/0 IRIS PURPLE MATTE (TOHO brand color name)
ANTENNAE: 15/0 BLACK OP

Approximate Finished Size: 3" x 2.25" (76mm x 57mm)

Section 1:

Work Section 1 from the bottom up following the diagram below. Match the increases (marked by < or >) and decreases to the diagram. Work the first four rows all the way across and then work the wing tips and body separately.

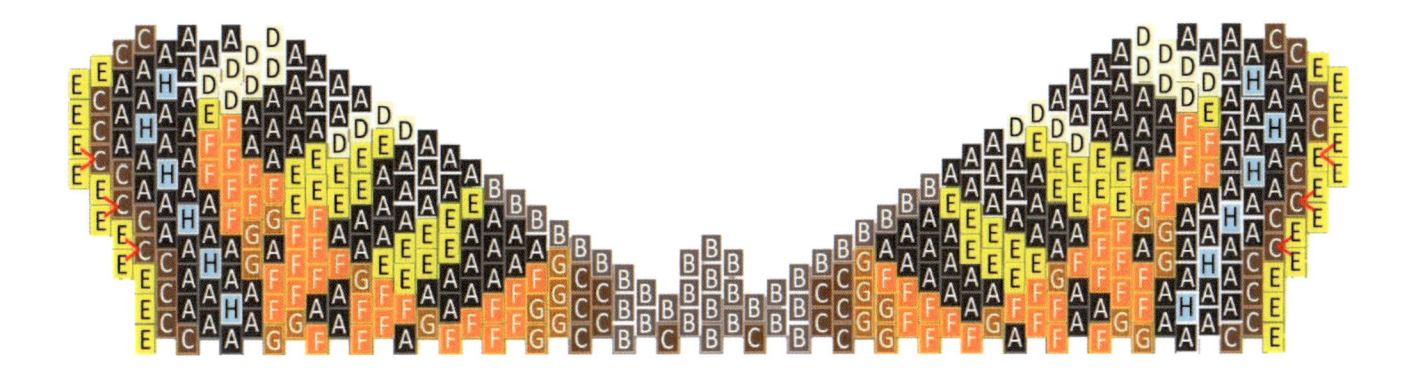

Section 2:

Turn Section 1 over and work Section 2 into the first row of Section 1 following the diagram below. Match decreases to the diagram.

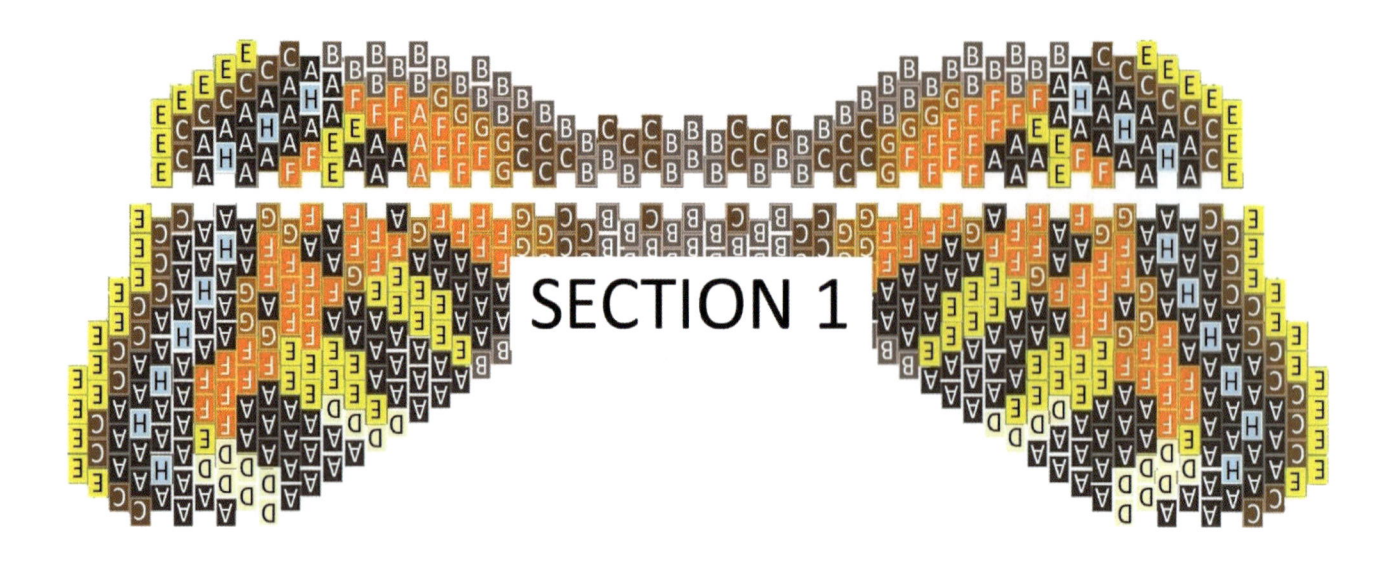

Section 3:

Work Section 3 from the bottom up following the diagram below.   Match decreases to the diagram.

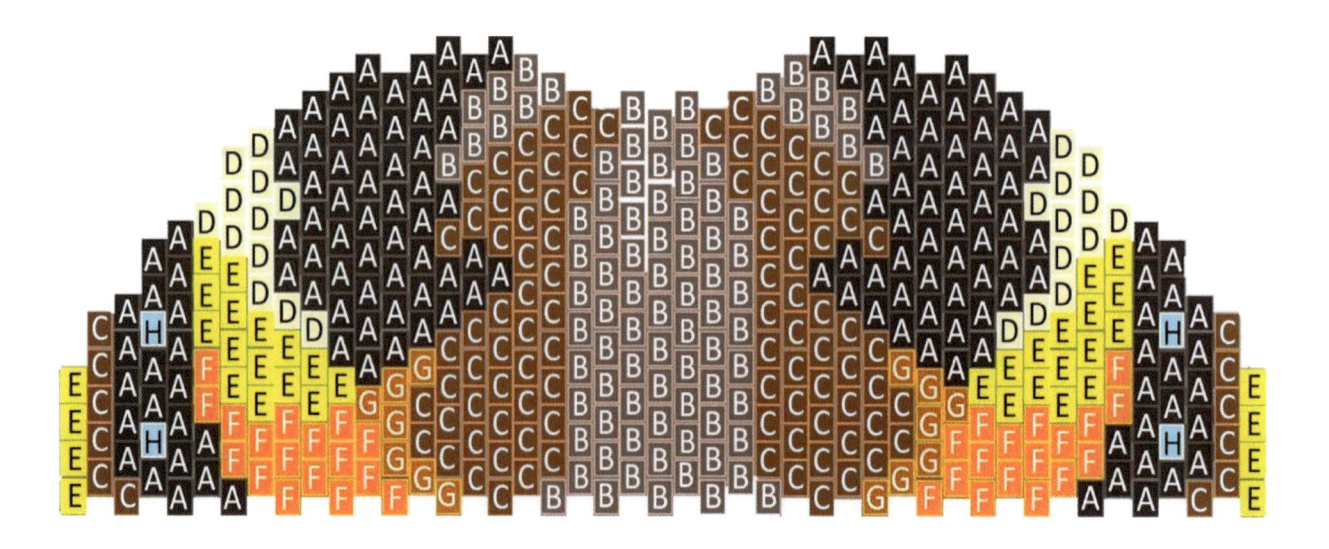

Section 4:

Turn Section 3 over and work Section 4 directly into the first row of Section 3 following the diagram below. Match decreases to the diagram.

Finish (refer to Chapter 1, if needed):

When both halves are finished, line up the two halves and sew them together at the body. Be careful to only sew the center three beads from each half.

Add a new thread:

Work the 3-D body from the tail end to the head end.
Finish with the antennae.

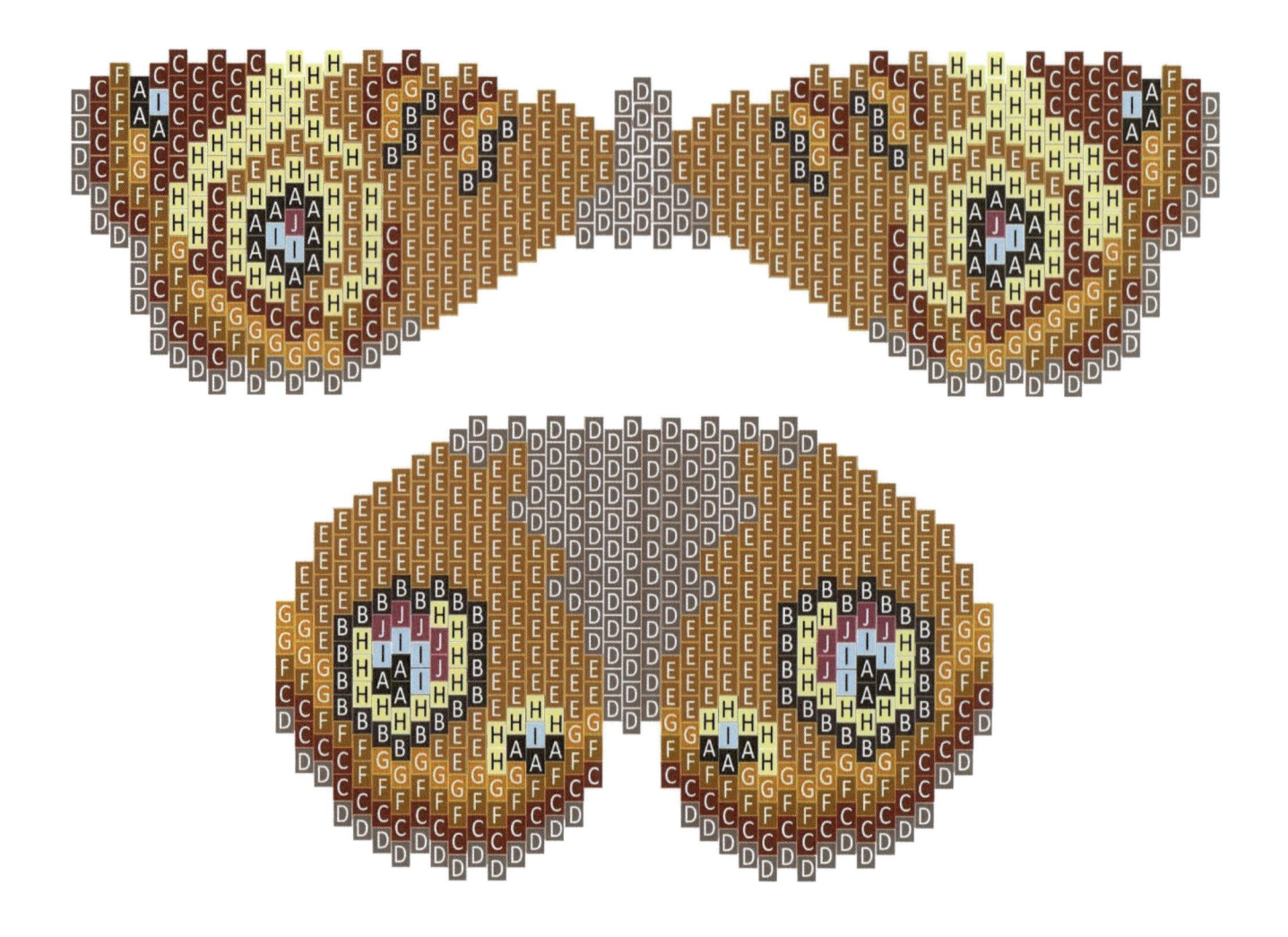

The Buckeye, or Common Buckeye, is an American butterfly ranging from southern Canada, through much of the United States and down into Central America.

Buckeye
(Junonia Coenia)

Materials:

Japanese Cylinder Beads

	Color #	Color Name	# of Beads
A	DB0010	Black: OP	33
B	DB0310	Black :OP MAT	56
C	DB1584	Reddish Brown: OP MAT	140
D	DB0735	Milk Chocolate Dk: OP	204
E	DB0853	Copper Md: TR MAT AB	340
F	DB2108	Copper: OP DURACOAT	66
G	DB2103	Yellow Marigold: OP DURA	66
H	DB2101	Pale Yellow: OP DURACOAT	116
I	DB1784	Baby Blue: WID	16
J	DB2118	Rose: OP DURACOAT	12

BODY: 15/0 IRIS PURPLE METALLIC FR (TOHO brand color name)
ANTENNAE: 15/0 CREAM

Approximate Finished Size: 3" x 1.75" (76mm x 44mm)

Section 1:

Work Section 1 from the bottom up following the diagram below. Match decreases to the diagram.

Section 2:

Turn Section 1 over and work Section 2 directly into the first row of Section 1 following the diagram below. Match decreases to the diagram. Only the first four rows are worked all the way across.

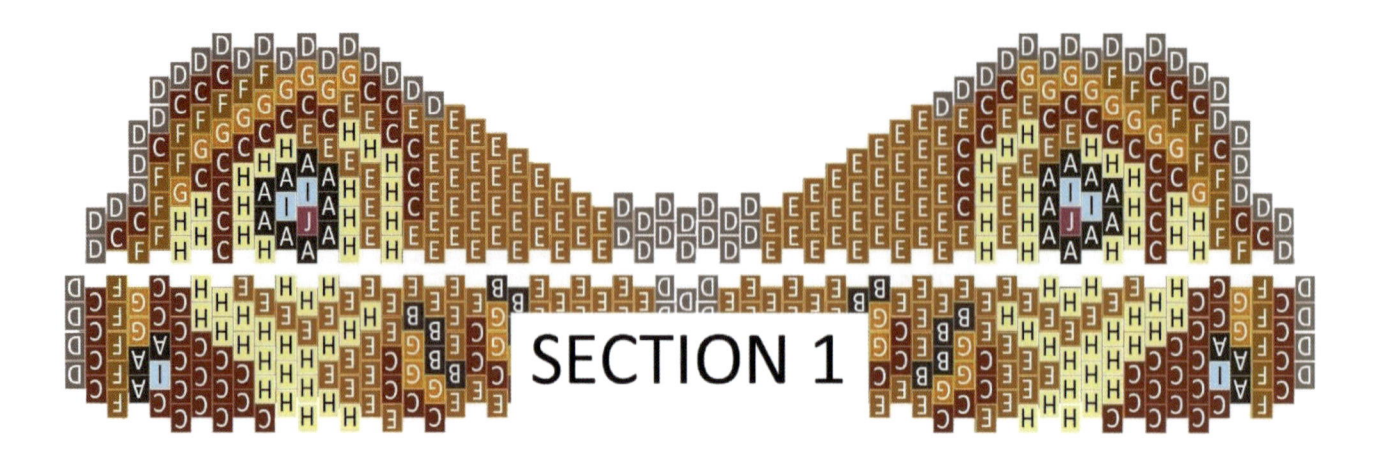

Section 3:

Work Section 3 from the bottom up following the diagram below. Match decreases to the diagram.

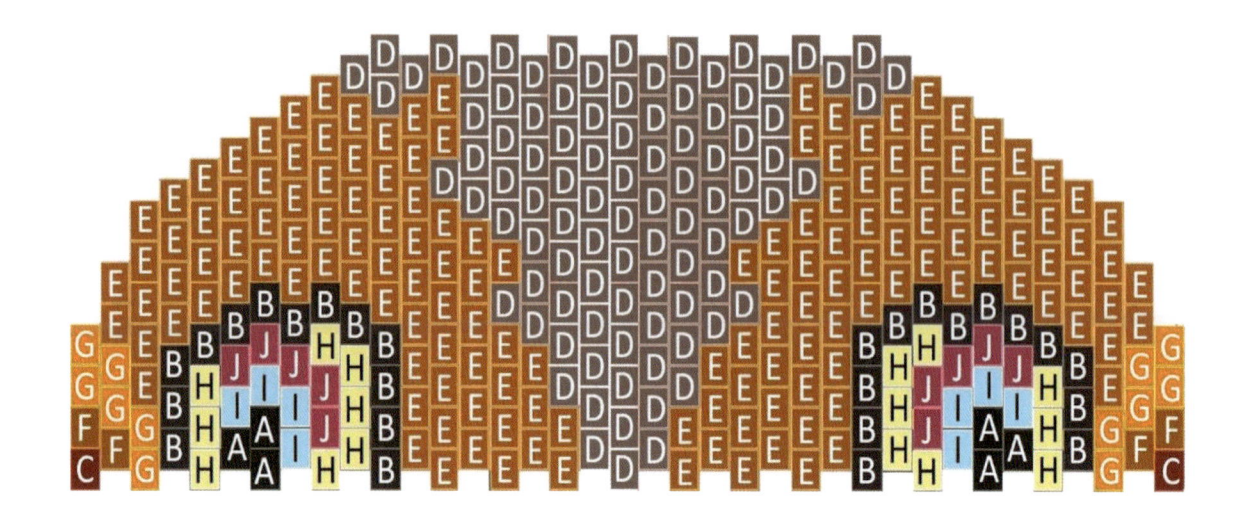

Section 4:

Turn Section 3 over and work section 4 directly into Section 3 following the diagram below. Note that only one row is worked all the way across and then each wing tip is worked separately. Match decreases to the diagram.

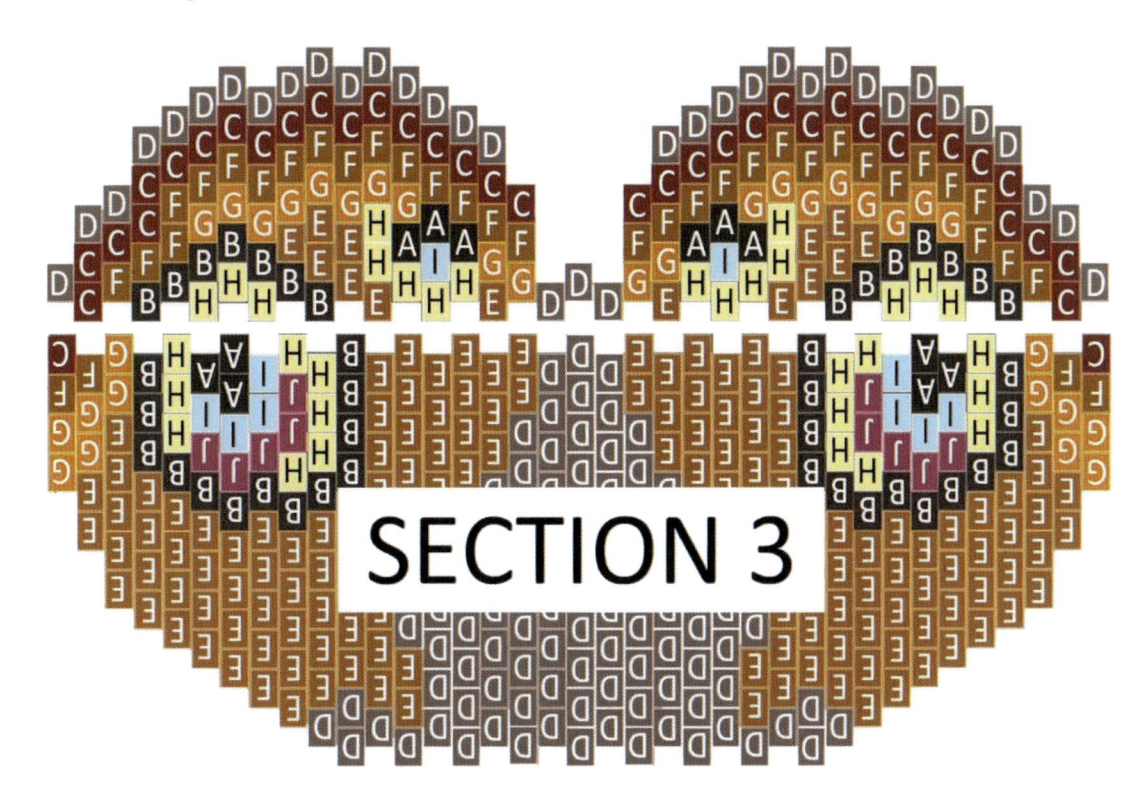

Finish (refer to Chapter 1, if needed):

When both halves are finished, line up the two halves and sew them together at the body. Be careful to only sew the center three beads from each half.

Add a new thread:

Work the 3-D body from the tail end to the head end.
Finish with the antennae.

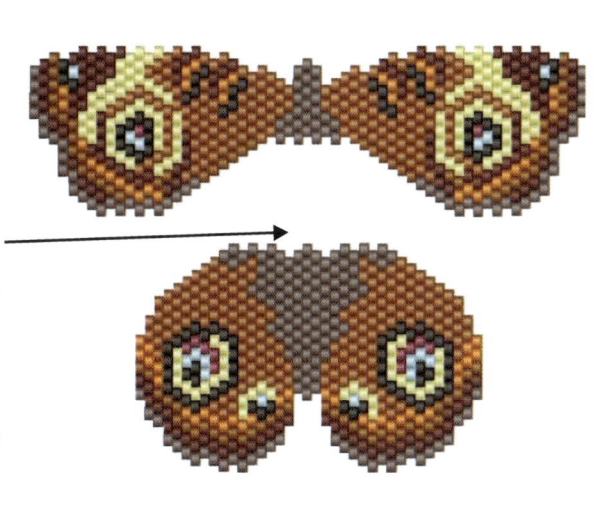

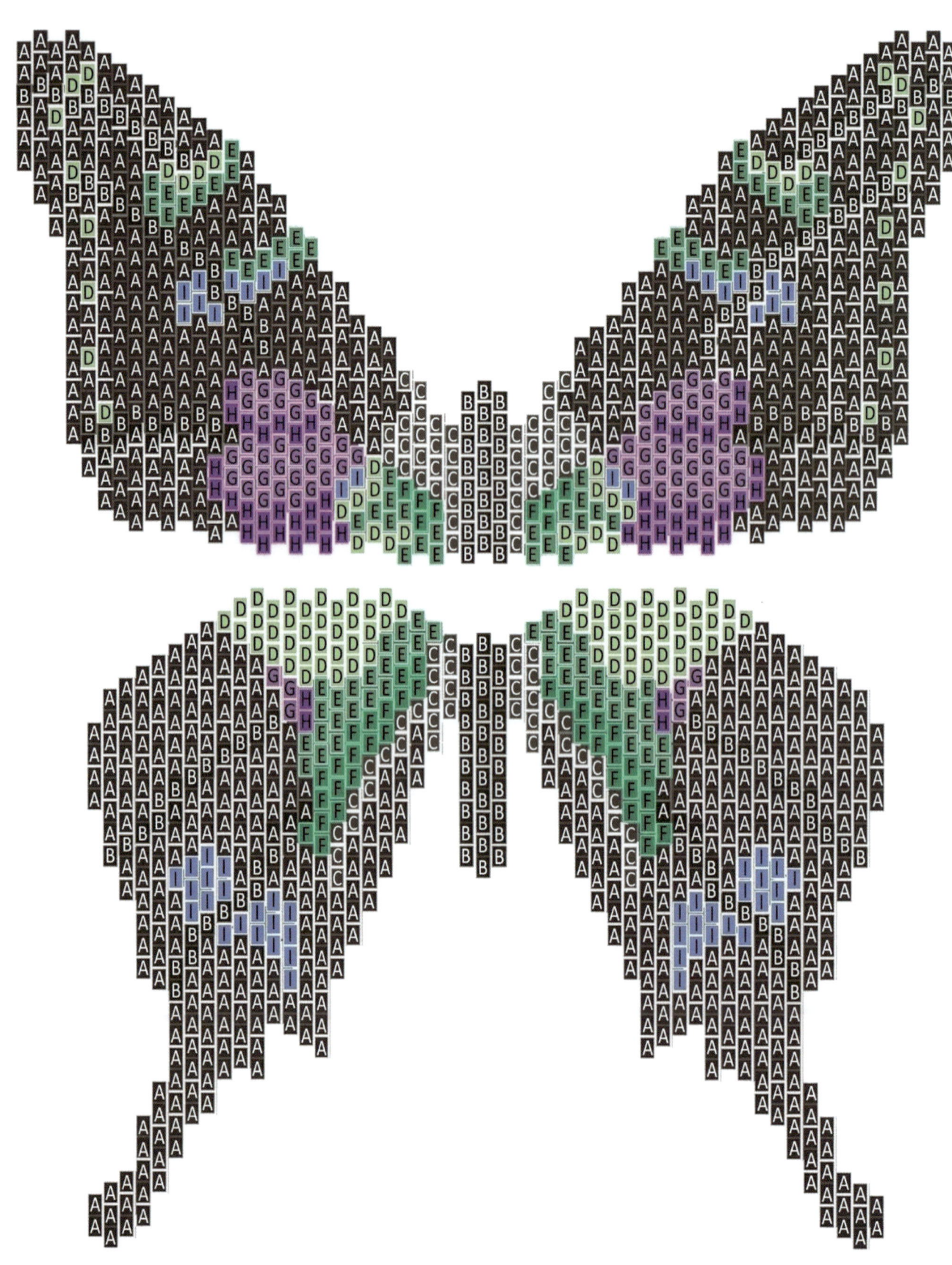

The Purple Spotted Swallowtail is most likely to be found in Papua New Guinea.

Purple Spotted Swallowtail
(Graphium Weiske)

Materials:

Japanese Cylinder Beads

	Color #	Color Name	# of Beads
A	DB0310	Black: MATTE	911
B	DB0010	Black: OP	176
C	DB0325	Teal Dk: MET MAT AB	82
D	DB2129	Cyan Blue Lt: OP DURA	110
E	DB2131	Cyan Blue Dk: OP DURA	96
F	DB2127	Green: OP DURACOAT	44
G	DB2138	Orchid Lt: OP DURACOAT	72
H	DB2140	Orchid Dk: OP DURACOAT	52
I	DB0760	Periwinkle: OP MAT	62

BODY: 15/0 IRIS PURPLE MATALLIC FR (TOHO brand)
ANTENNAE: 15/0 BLACK: OP

Approximate Finished Size: 3" x 3.5" (76mm x 89mm)

Section 1:

Work Section 1 from the bottom up following the diagram below. Match decreases to the diagram.

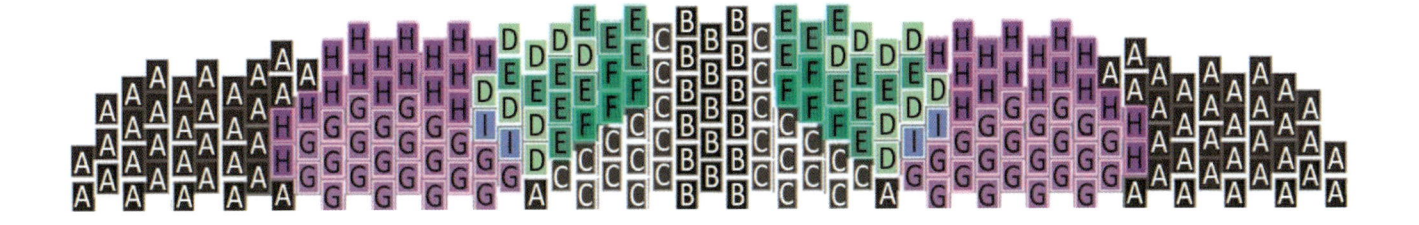

Section 2:

Turn Section 1 over and work Section 2 directly into Section 1 following the diagram below. Work the first two rows of Section 2 all the way across, then work each part separately. Match the increases and decreases to the diagram. Note that there is an increase off the 2nd row on the outside edge of each wing.

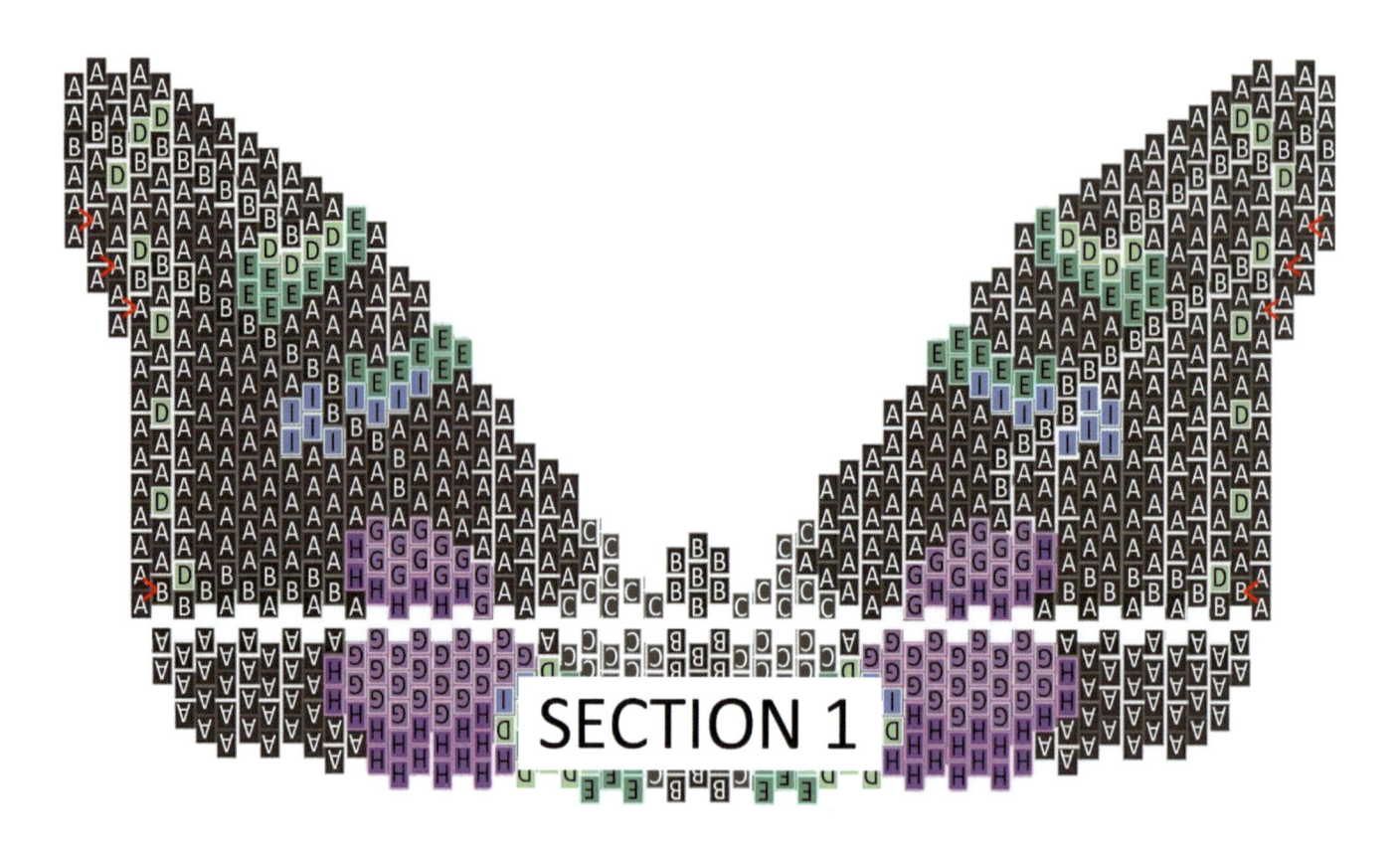

Section 3:

Work Section 3 from the bottom up following the diagram below. Match decreases to the diagram.

38

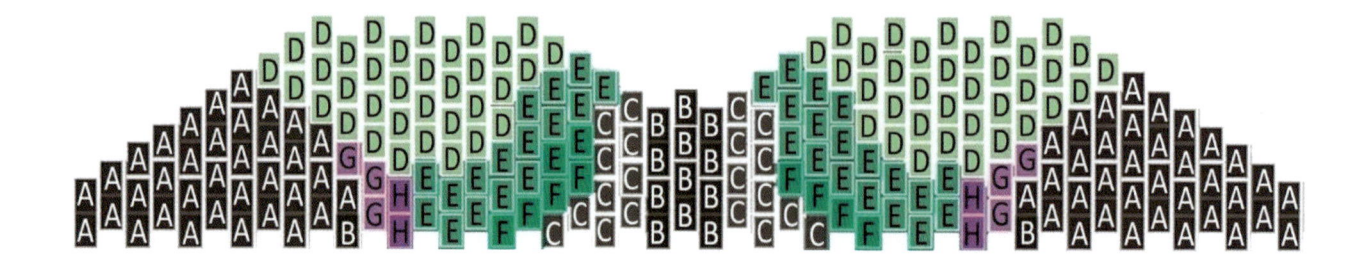

Section 4:

Turn Section 3 over and work Section 4 directly into the first row of Section 3 following the diagram below. Work the two wing sections but do not work the body area just yet. Match increases and decreases to the diagram. Note that there is an increase on the 2nd row.

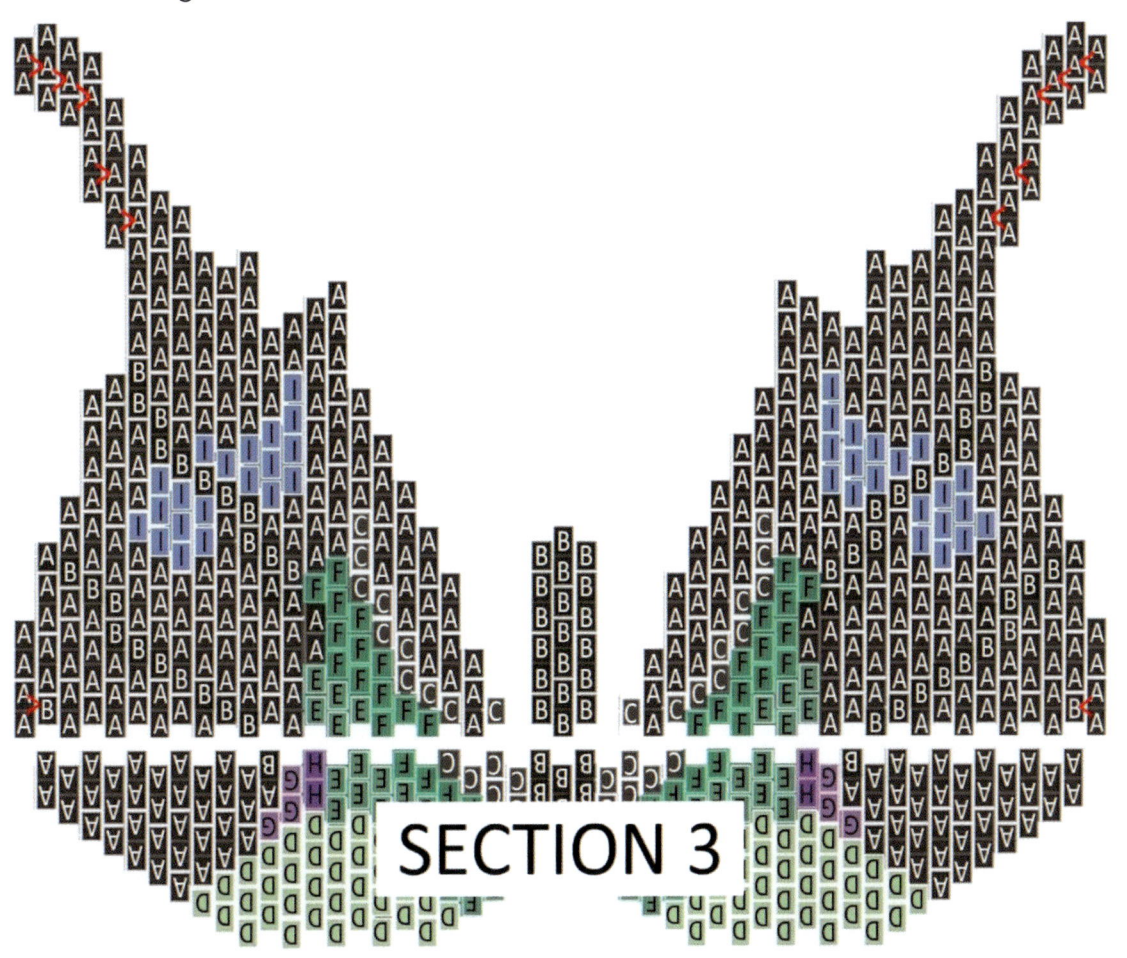

Finish (refer to Chapter 1, if needed):

When both halves are finished except for the tail end of the body, line up the two halves and sew them together at the body. Be careful to only sew the center three beads from each half.

Add a new thread:
1. work the end of the base layer of the body from the wings down to the tail end
2. work the 3-D body from the tail end to the head end.
3. finish with the antennae.

The Danube Clouded Yellow butterfly can be found in western Asia and eastern Europe but has become endangered in central Europe.

Danube Clouded Yellow
(Colias Myrmidone)

Materials:

Japanese Cylinder Beads

	Color #	Color Name	# of Beads
A	DB0310	Black: OP MAT	240
B	DB1786	Avocado Lt: WID	61
C	DB0733	Chartreuse: OP	38
D	DB1582	Lemon: OP MAT	294
E	DB2103	Yellow Marigold: OP DURA	260
F	DB2104	Cheddar Orange: OP DURA	72

BODY: 15/0 IRIS BROWN MATTE (TOHO brand shown)
ANTENNAE: BLACK MATTE

Approximate Finished Size: 2.5" x 1 7/8" (63mm x 48mm)

Section 1:

Work Section 1 from the bottom up following the diagram below. Work the first three rows all the way across and then work each wing separately. Match the decreases and increases to the diagram. Only the first three rows run all the way across.

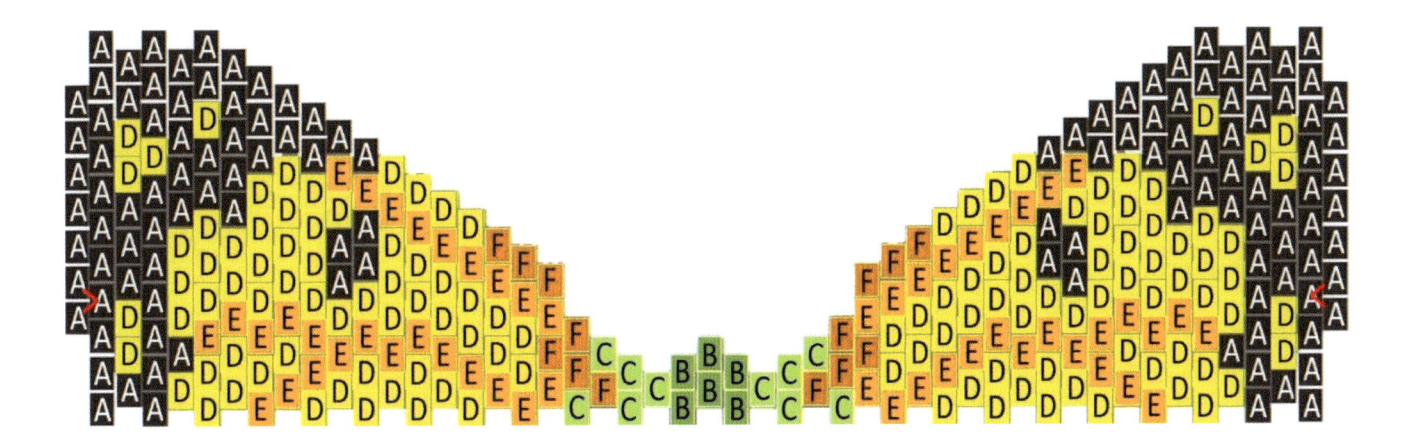

Section 2:

Turn Section 1 over and work Section 2 directly into the first row of Section 1 following the diagram below.

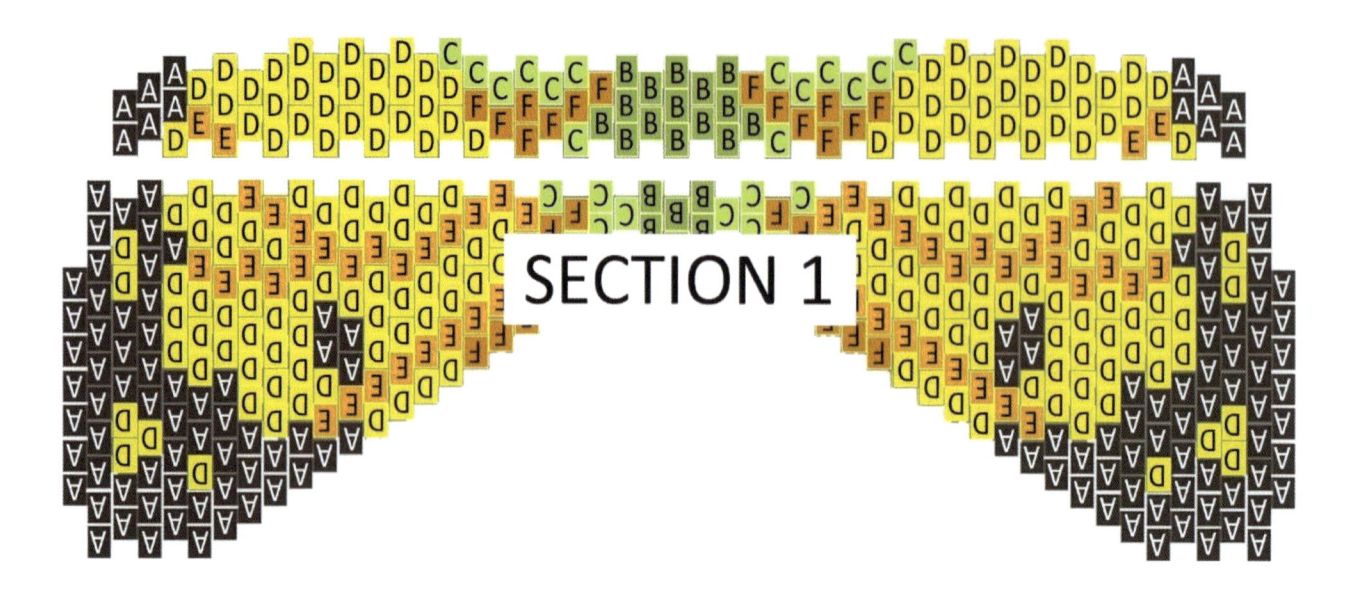

Section 3:

Work Section 3 from the bottom up following the diagram below. Match decreases to the diagram.

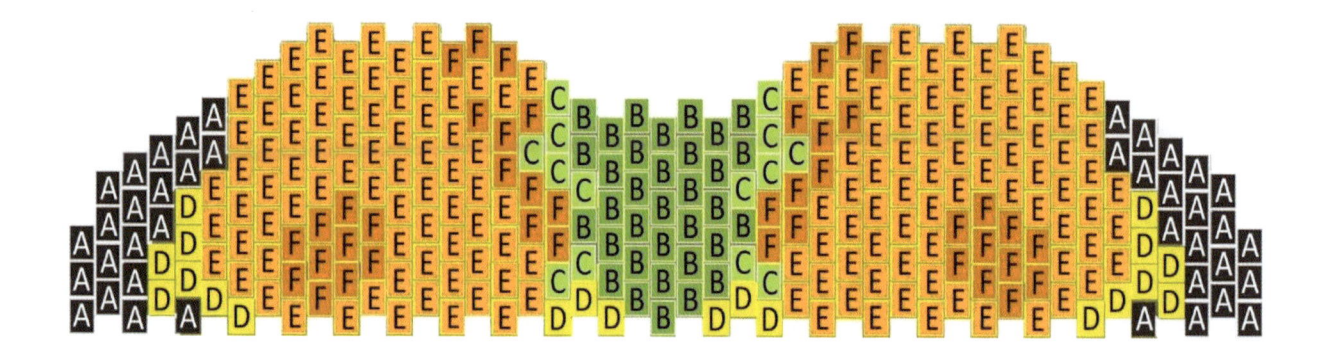

Section 4:

Turn Section 3 over and work Section 4 directly into the first row of Section 1 following the diagram below. Note that only the first row goes all the way across before working the wings separately. Leave off the center body section for now.

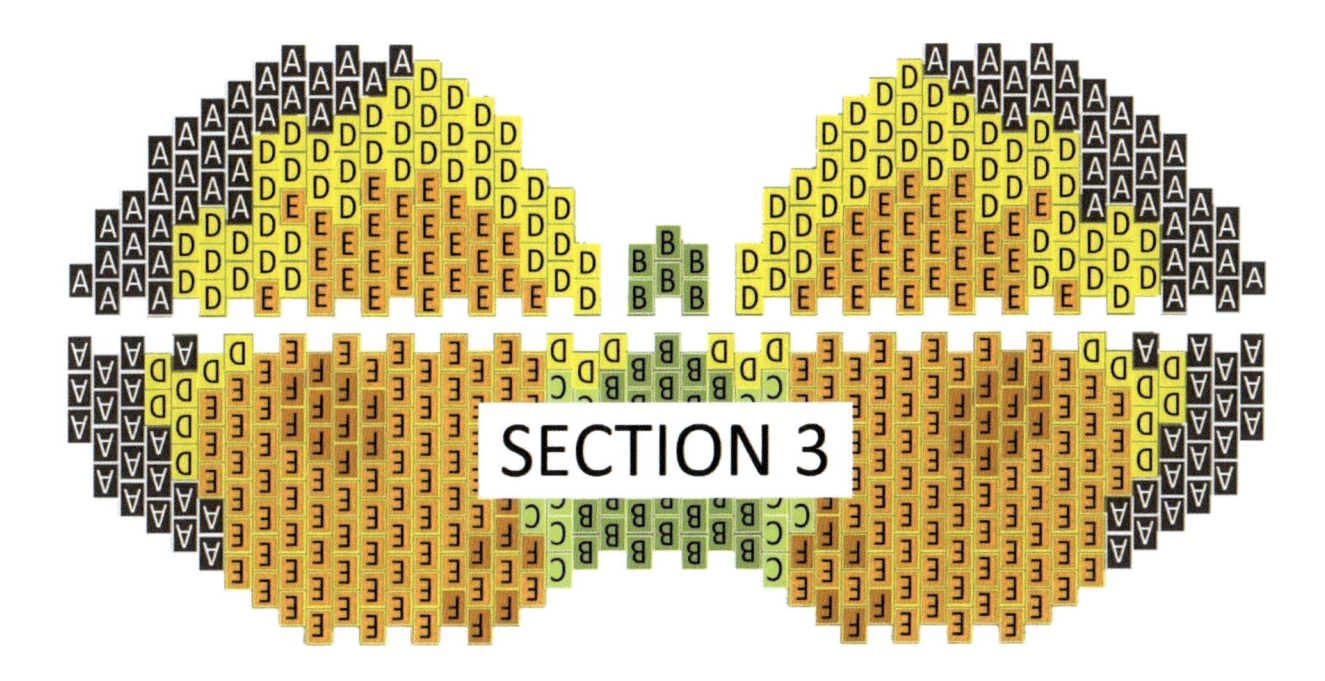

Finish (refer to Chapter 1, if needed):

When both halves are finished except for the tail end of the body, line up the two halves and sew them together at the body. Be careful to only sew the center three beads from each half.

Add a new thread:

1. work the end of the base layer of the body from the wings down to the tail end
2. work the 3-D body from the tail end to the head end.
3. finish with the antennae.

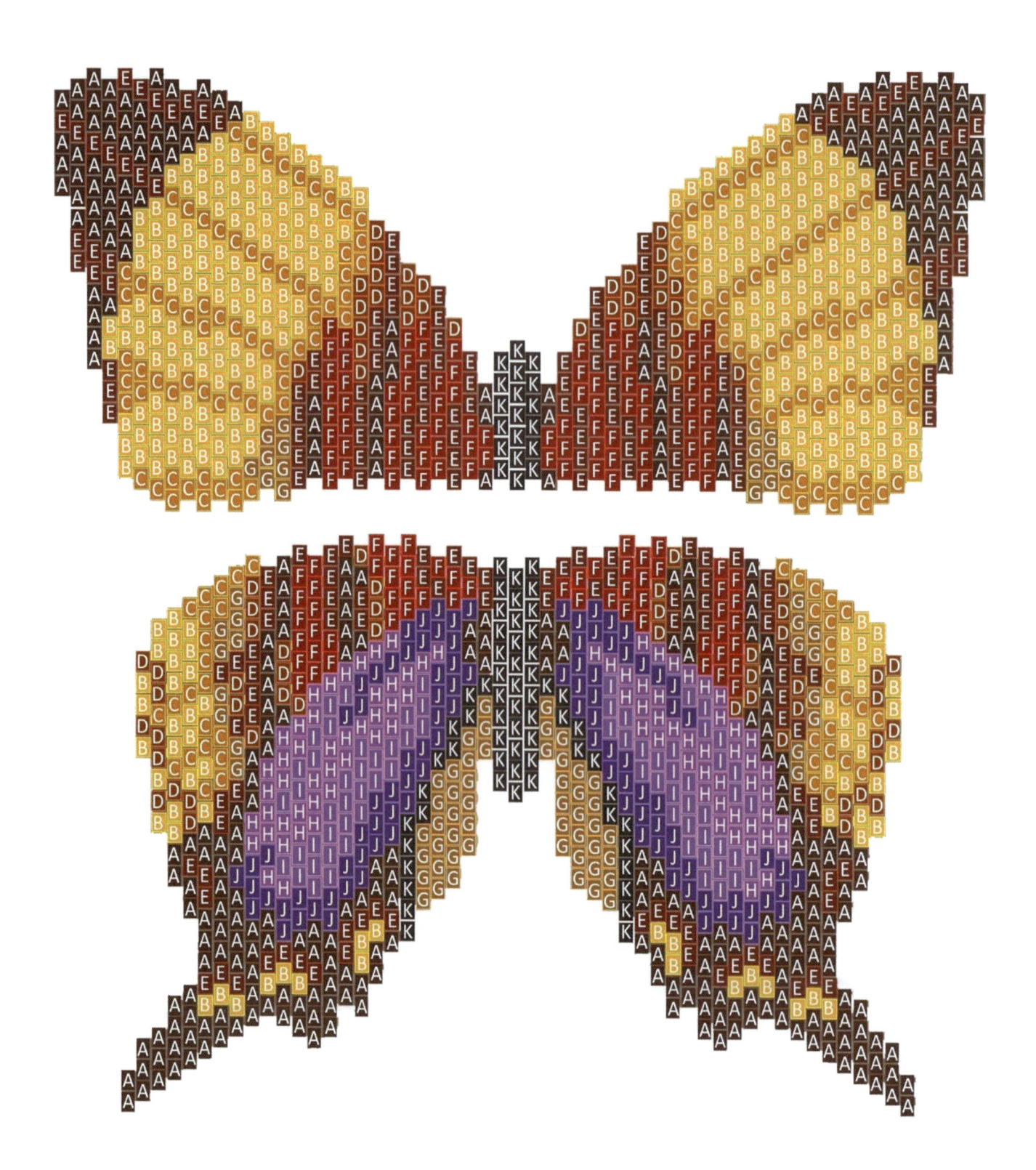

The Corinna Daggertail is native to the eastern Andes of South America from Columbia to Peru. They can be either purple and yellow as shown here, or they may be more blue and orange.

Corinna Daggertail

(Marpesia Corinna)

Materials:

Japanese Cylinder Beads

	Color #	Color Name	# of Beads
A	DB0007	Brown Dk: MET IRIS	352
B	DB2103	Yellow Marigold: OP DURA	338
C	DB2104	Cheddar Orange: OP DURA	178
D	DB2108	Copper: OP DURACOAT	84
E	DB0734	Mahogany Dk: OP	203
F	DB2120	Maroon Dk: OP DURACOAT	141
G	DB0853	Copper Md: TR MAT AB	80
H	DB2136	Dusty Lavender: OP DURA	86
I	DB2138	Orchid Lt: OP DURACOAT	70
J	DB2140	Orchid Dk: OP DURACOAT	100
K	DB0310	Black: OP MAT	80

BODY: 15/0 IRIS PURPLE METALLIC FR (TOHO brand shown)

ANTENNAE: 15/0 BLACK OP

Approximate Finished Size: 3" x 3 1/8" (76mm x 80mm)

Section 1:

Work Section 1 from the bottom up following the diagram below. Match increases and decreases to the diagram.

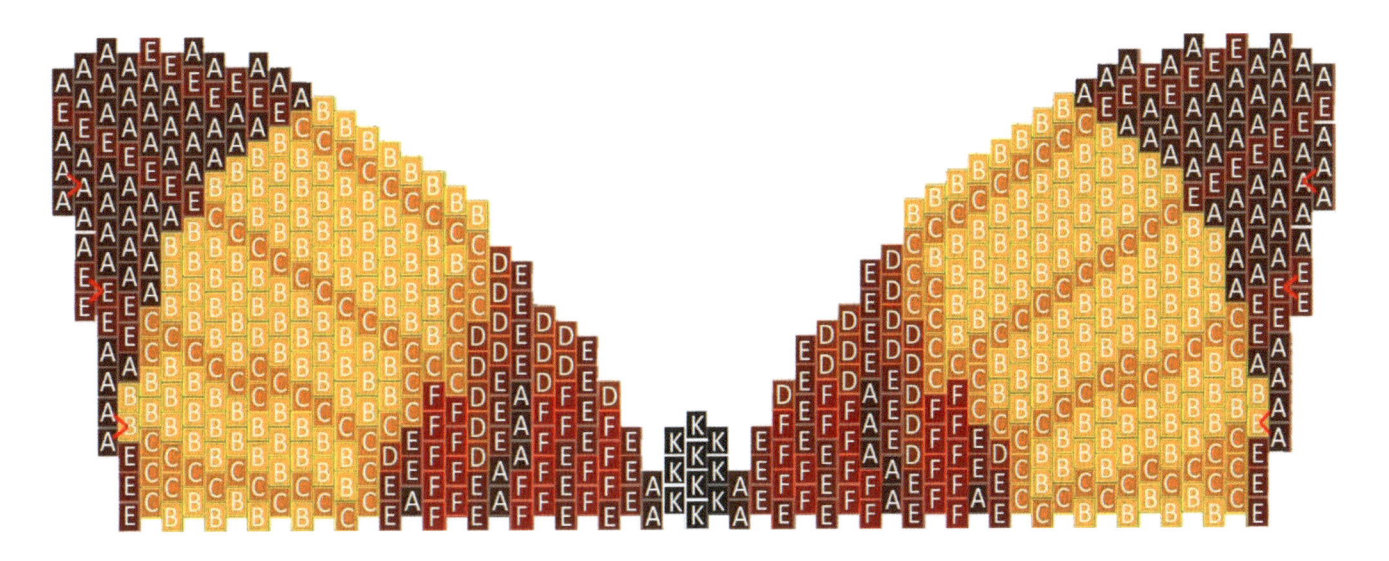

Section 2:

Turn Section 1 over and work Section 2 directly into the first row of Section 1 following the diagram below.

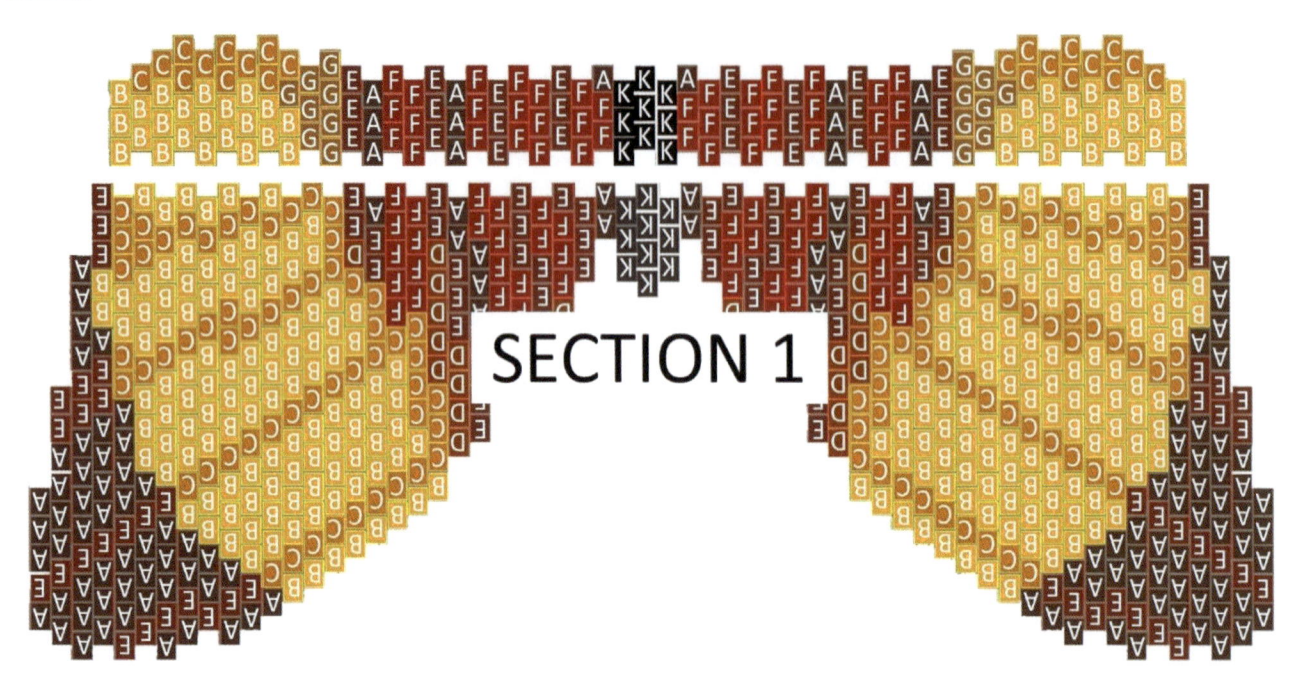

Section 3:

Work Section 3 from the bottom up following the diagram below. Match increases and decreases to the diagram. Work the wings and leave off the rest of the center body section for now.

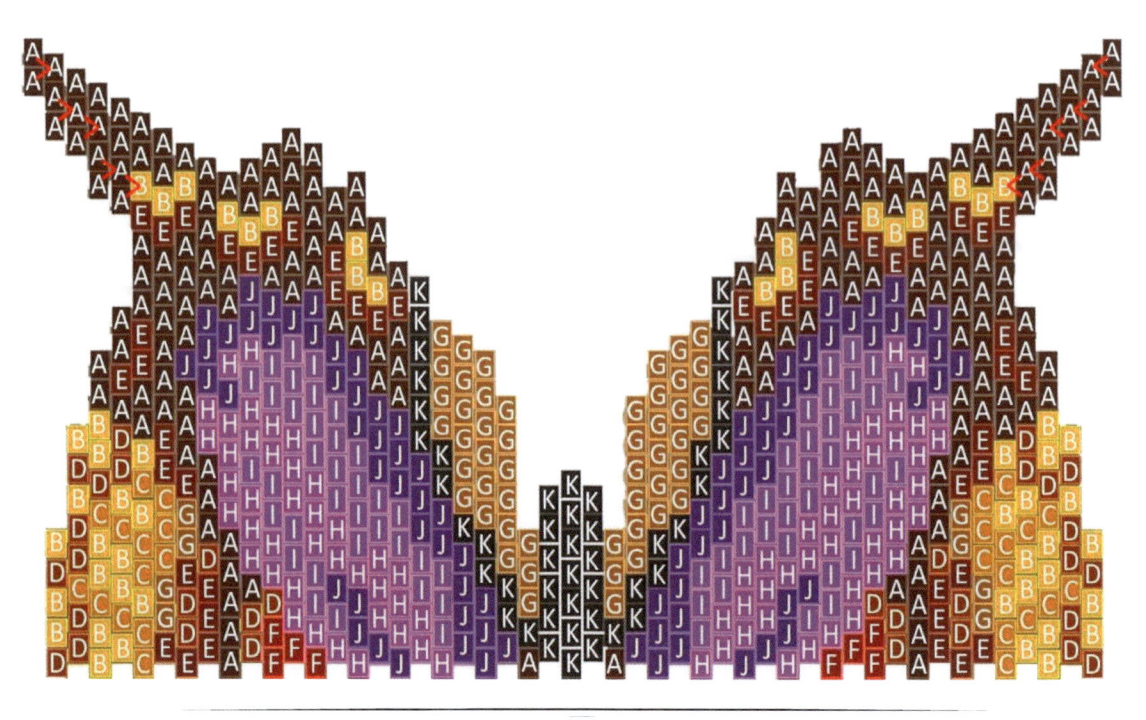

Section 4:

Turn Section 3 over and work Section 4 directly into the first row of Section 2 following the diagram below.

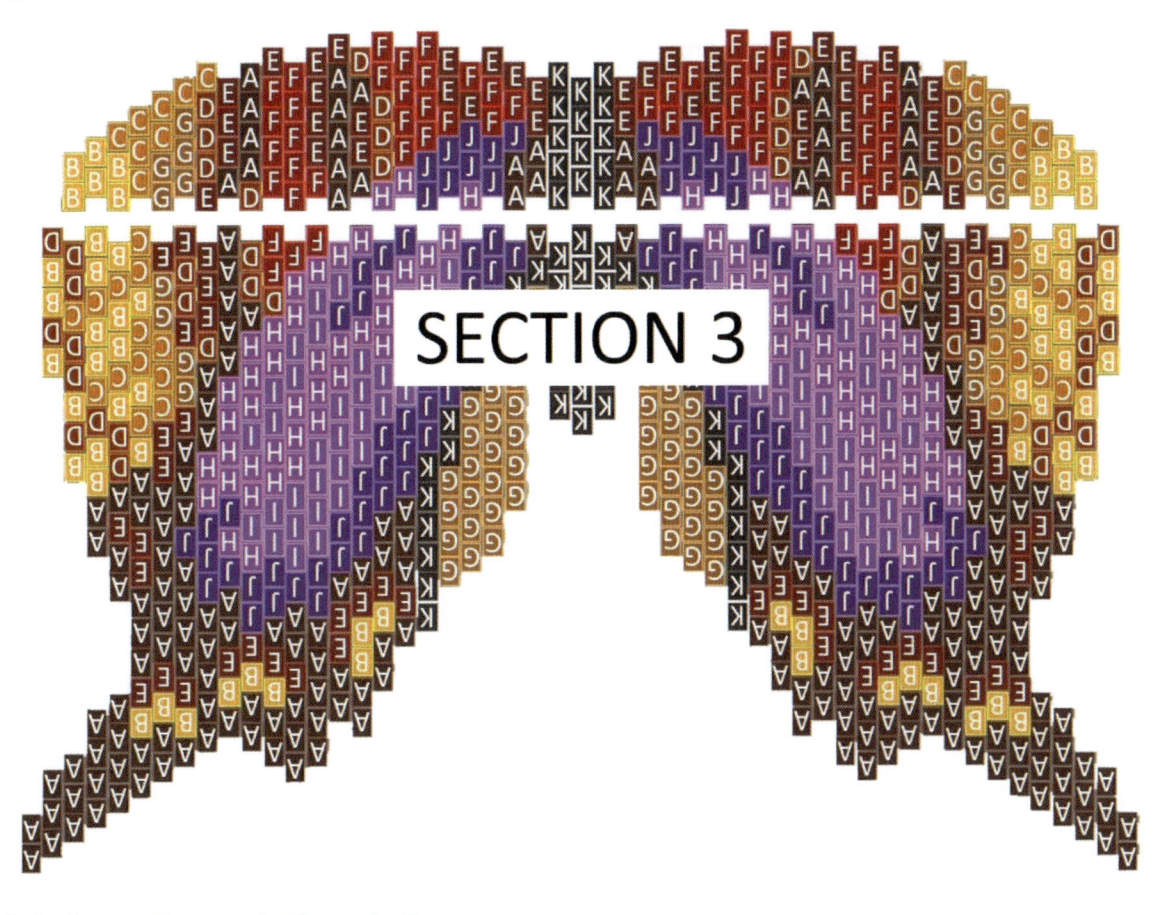

Finish (refer to Chapter 1, if needed):

When both halves are finished except for the tail end of the body, line up the two halves and sew them together at the body. Be careful to only sew the center three beads from each half.

Add a new thread:
1. work the end of the base layer of the body from the wings down to the tail end
2. work the 3-D body from the tail end to the head end.
3. finish with the antennae.

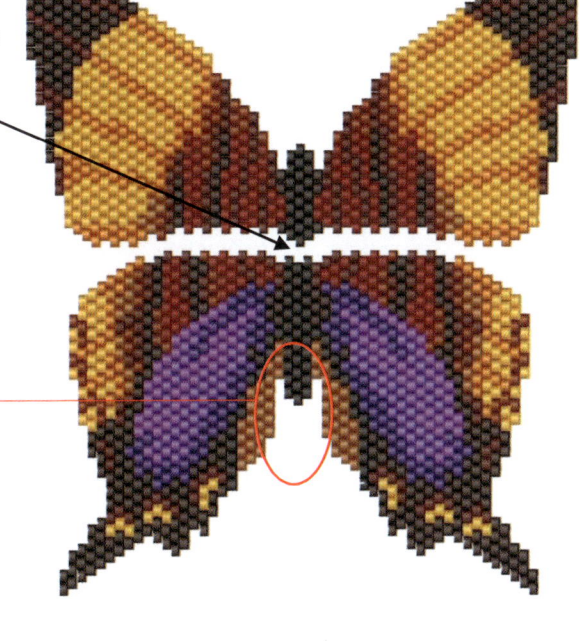

47

Necklace Centerpiece

Framed

Suggested Uses

Add a pin back for a broach
Add a hairclip backing
Sew onto your hat or purse
Decorate your denim jacket

Holiday Ornament

Printed in Great Britain
by Amazon